Tak Kak's *Liberty*

Tak Kak's *Liberty*

Letters and Essays by James L. Walker
for Benjamin R. Tucker's *Liberty*,
(1885–1903)

STAND ALONE

This volume presents every known contrubution by James L. Walker, and his alias "Tak Kak", to the journal *Liberty*. While often just a single voice excised from a larger conversation, the reader can find much of the source material online for context.

CONTENTS

A Southern Journalist's Opinion.............................7
Liberty, vol. 3 no. 19 (December 12, 1885): 5.
What is Justice?...8
Liberty, vol. 3 no. 25 (March 6, 1886): 8.
Killing Chinese..11
Liberty, vol. 3 no. 25 (March 6, 1886): 8.
Selfhood Terminates Blind Man's Buff.....................13
Liberty, vol. 4 no. 5 (July 3,1886): 8.
Egoism in Sexual Relations..............................15
Liberty, vol. 4 no. 6 (July 17, 1886): 5.
Regicides and Republicans..............................16
Liberty, vol. 4 no. 11 (November 20, 1886): 5.
The Colin Campbell Suit................................18
Liberty, vol. 4 no. 13 (January 1, 1887): 4.
The Rational Utilitarian Philosophy.....................19
Liberty, vol. 4 no. 13 (January 22, 1887): 8.
Proudhon's Works a Source of Health.....................20
Liberty, vol. 4 no. 16 (February 26, 1887): 1.
Truth and Belief.......................................21
Liberty, vol. 4 no. 17 (March 12, 1887): 7.
Stirner on Justice......................................22
Liberty, vol. 4 no. 18 (March 26, 1887): 7.
Egoism...25
Liberty, vol. 4 no. 19 (April 9, 1887): 5-7.
Reply to John F. Kelly..................................38
Liberty, vol. 4 no. 24 (July 2, 1887): 7.
On Mr. Kelly's Final Statement..........................45
Liberty, vol. 5 no. 1 (August 13, 1887): 5.
Noms de Plume...51
Liberty, vol. 5 no. 1 (August 27, 1887): 5.
Edgeworth's Miserable Insinuations......................52
Liberty, vol. 5 no. 4 (September 24, 1887): 5.
Anarchy, Government, and Liberty........................53
Liberty, vol. 5 no. 6 (October 22, 1887): 6.
A Reason for Hanging Anarchists.........................56
Liberty, vol. 5 no. 11 (December 31, 1887): 4.
Self-Wisdom and Egoism.................................57
Liberty, vol. 5 no. 11 (December 31, 1887): 6.
Egoism and Selfishness.................................59
Liberty, vol. 5 no. 16 (March 10, 1888): 5.

A Difference of Words Only. 61
   Liberty, vol. 5 no. 17 (March 31, 1888): 7.
A Normal Function. 62
   Liberty, vol. 5, no. 26 (August 4, 1888): 5.
Even So, What Then? 63
   Liberty, vol. 7 no. 2 (May 24, 1890): 3.
Tak Kak Not with the "Brave." 64
   Liberty, vol. 7 no. 4 (June 21, 1890): 7.
The Question of Copyright.—I. 65
   Liberty, vol. 7 no. 22 (February 21, 1891): 5.
Hare and Tortoise. 68
   Liberty, vol. 7 no. 22 (February 21, 1891): 7.
Sentimental and Incomplete. 69
   Liberty, vol. 7 no. 23 (March 7, 1891): 1.
Copyright.—II. 72
   Liberty, vol. 7 no. 23 (March 7, 1891): 5–6.
Copyright.—III. 75
   Liberty, vol. 7 no. 24 (March 21, 1891): 4–5.
A Century of Fraud.. 82
   Liberty, vol. 8 no. 11 (August 22, 1891): 3.
Must the Ego Count Himself Out? 83
   Liberty, vol. 8 no. 25 (November 28, 1891): 3.
Egoism or Self-Sacrifice? 86
   Liberty, vol. 8 no. 36 (February 13, 1892): 2–3.
Wiles of the Social Man. 92
   Liberty, vol. 8 no. 38 (May 7, 1892): 2.
Monopoly's Devious Ways.. 95
   Liberty, vol. 9 no. 29 (March 18, 1893): 3.
Spencer and George.— I. 98
   Liberty, vol. 9 no. 31 (April 1, 1893): 2.
Spencer and George.—II. 101
   Liberty, vol. 9 no. 34 (April 22, 1893): 2–3.
Spencer and George.—III. 106
   Liberty, vol. 9 no. 38 (May 20, 1893): 2.
Cleveland's Commission. 109
   Liberty, vol. 9 no. 51 (April 21, 1894): 2–3.
A Pointer for Trade Unions. 112
   Liberty, vol. 14 no. 12 (August, 1903): 4.
"Representative" Government.. 115
   Liberty, vol. 14 no. 13 (September, 1903): 4.
The Virus of Specific Moralism. 117
   Liberty, vol. 14 no. 14 (October, 1903): 7.

A Southern Journalist's Opinion.

Liberty, vol. 3 no. 19 (December 12, 1885): 5.

Dear Mr. Tucker:

I am delighted with every issue of your paper. Your reply to Edgeworth on the question of rent is very just.

J. L. WALKER.

Galveston, Texas, October 11, 1885.

What is Justice?
Liberty, vol. 3 no. 25 (March 6, 1886): 8.

It is an idea presupposing a power that lays down a rule or law
to which the individual owes respect and obedience. God is
presented as the supreme egoist. My wishes must yield to his.
This is God's justice or law. Those who believe in God fear
and obey, — not I. Then comes society's justice. "Society," the
egoist, orders what it wills. I must sacrifice my wishes to the
family, to the State, to humanity. If the power exists and knows
how to subject me, I must, — not otherwise. Shall I waste my
life in setting up and obeying an idea that I must treat all men
alike? They are not alike, — not equally able or willing to sustain me in return. Society is the natural state of men, and holds
each individual to "duties" so long as it can, or till he refuses
to obey. When he comes to mil consciousness, he sets up as
his own master, and thereafter, if there is to be any use for the
word justice, it must mean the rules of a union of egoists with
benefits to at least balance duties; and these duties are simply
matter of contract. The egoists will act as they see fit or prudent toward natural society. Can any infidel say why he directly
enslaves horses and not men? Men are indirectly enslaved, and
their deference to ideas keeps them enslaved. It is useless to
urge that slavery is unjust. The chameleon changes color, but
remains a chameleon. One form of slavery is abolished to give
place to another so long as men consent to be held subject.
The idea that slavery is "unjust" is the idea that there is a rule
or law against it. The facts of nature are there. The mere idea
that, if rulers would cease to oppress, all would be better, is not
effective of improvement to the subject man. When, however,
it comes to his consciousness that he is naturally a subject till
he refuses, and realizes that power and will are the essential
matters, he makes himself free so far as he can. It is "just" to
enslave those willing to be enslaved,—that is, it is according
to the rule, or law, or shortest line of nature. Those who believe that man has an immortal soul, and that a horse has not,
may act from superstitious fear or reverence. The intelligent
egoist will "respect" the "vicious" horse sooner than the tame,
subservient man. Viciousness is the resistance to enslavement.

There is more virtue in the criminal classes than in the tame slaves. Crime and virtue are the same under State tyranny, as sin and virtue are the same under theological tyranny. "Justice," as a generality, with reference to natural society, is a snare, or a transposition of the horse and cart. I recognize no duty toward the powers that control me instead of bargaining with me. I am indifferent to the annihilation of the serfs whose consent enslaves me along with themselves. I am at war with natural society, and "all's fair" in war, although all is not expedient. All was lawful, but not expedient, with the apostle. So it is with the individual come to self-consciousness, not for the Lord's sake or humanity's sake, but for himself. The assertion of himself will be as general and various as his faculties'. To utterly dismiss the idea that there is any other justice in nature than force seeking the least line of resistance is to dismiss at the same time the idea that there is any injustice. This may save generations of complaining and begging. In short, we want to perceive the facts and processes of nature without colored glass before our eyes. No justice, no injustice, as between an individual and any other in nature? Why then no wrong in any method of becoming free! Startling thought to the halting slave! Nothing in crime but a fact? Nothing. See the complaining wife, not loving, but submitting and suffering. Nothing wrong in putting six inches of steel into the bosom of her liege lord? The egoist says, call it what you like, there is no hell. What the woman will do depends upon what are her thoughts. Therefore, my reader, as the laws of society, and the State, one of its forms, are tyrannies or disagreeable impediments to me (but I need not give any reason except to influence yon), and I see no difficulty in discarding them but your respect for ideas such as "right," "wrong," "justice," etc., I would have you consider that these are merely words with vague, chimerical meanings, as there is no moral government of the world, but merely an evolutionary process, and it depends upon perception of this fact, and self-direction of our individual powers united as we shall agree, how we can succeed in obtaining and enjoying more or less of the things of this world. Do yon feel fully conscious of this? Then you and I can perhaps join our forces, and I begin to have an appreciable interest in you. Nothing that I could do for you (without setting you in power over myself) could fail to be agreeable to me. I think we will not act very benevolently toward outsiders. They might take all we offered, as the ox takes the grass in his pasture. Disinterestedness is said to feed on unreciprocating self-indulgence in those upon whom it is spent. Do you not begin to think that by suiting only myself I am really doing far better toward others than by throwing myself away to serve them? If so, it is a lucky coincidence, for I only serve and amuse myself. And I really do not care if you call that unjust. I shall begin to work for you when I see yon are able to work for me. But if you are afraid to be free,—stay in slavery. I must have the satisfaction of seeing that you do not wholly escape suffering, if you are so unfit to aid me when I would aid you. And if you are thus lacking in stamina or sense, it will be no harm if you do get overworked and your existence is shortened. But I hope better things from you.

TAK KAK.

Killing Chinese.

Liberty, vol. 3 no. 25 (March 6, 1886): 8.

I do not question that the willing white slaves of America are capable of multiplying till they can supply the labor market as cheaply as Chinese now do. But the slaves who know that they are slaves, and who are not superstitious about killing a man, may prefer that whites shall be here rather than Chinamen. The Chinaman is a sort of man more fitted by nature and heredity to remain a slave than the Caucasian. The Caucasian as yet acts in slavish submission to his master, but discovers the other side of his character when he meets the Chinese slave or Chinese master. This shocks Gertrude B. Kelly, who is a victim of the fixed idea that all men are brothers,—a poetical fragment dissociated from and surviving the idea of the fatherhood of God. For my part I do not think that any white working people in America will be worse off because there are some dead Chinamen where there were some living ones. When the whites come to understand things better, it is very probable that there will be some dead white men under similar circumstances. I shall not pretend to tell anybody what he ought to do, at least not until I am in some sort of association with him under a mutual agreement.

Tak Kak.

[It will be seen that "Tak Kak," in his two articles, defends or apologizes for the killing of Chinamen upon the ground that there are no obligations upon human beings in their relations with each other, except those that are made such by mutual agreement. Very well. But do all agreements, to be binding, hare to be signed and sealed, or even written? Not at all. There is a tacit agreement or understanding between human beings, not as brothers,—and I do not think that Miss Kelly intended to use the word "brothers" in any sentimental sense,—but as individuals living in daily contact and dependent upon some sort of cooperation with each other for the satisfaction of their daily wants, not to trespass upon each other's individuality, the motive of this agreement being the purely egoistic desire of each for the peaceful preservation of his own individuality. Now it is true that, while almost all men recognize in the abstract the binding force of this agreement, the great majority of them either wilfully violate it, believing themselves strong enough to do so with impunity and with benefit to themselves, or ignorantly violate it through mistaken and superstitious ideas about religion, morality, and duty, and so commit trespass upon the individualities of others. All such men, I agree with "Tak Kak," whether their skins be yellow or white or black, may properly be forced, by those who are disposed to abide by this agreement, to pay whatever penalty the latter may deem it necessary or wise to inflict. Such men, be their names Jay Gould, Grover Cleveland, Alexander III., Bill Sykes, or Ah Sing, are outlaws, rebels not necessarily against statute law but against the true law of human relationships, and, being outlaws, may be treated as such. But to make these men pay the penalties of their trespasses is a very different thing from killing Chinamen who have done nothing more heinous than to make their own contracts. If it is a trespass on A's individuality for B to offer his labor in the market at a lower price than A sets on his, then indeed we are all trespassers, for every act of every one of us is liable to affect in some minute way the welfare of every other; and in that case there is no possibility of peaceful preservation of individualities, the alternative being a permanent state of internecine war or the absolutism of the Czar of Russia. So as many "dead white men," or dead yellow men, as you please, "Tak Kak," provided they have been trespassers; and neither Miss Kelly nor myself will shed any tears over their graves. But both of us, I think, will continue to do all we can to prevent the killing of any men, white or yellow, who propose to mind their own business. — Editor *Liberty*.]

Selfhood Terminates Blind Man's Buff.

Liberty, vol. 4 no. 5 (July 3,1886): 8.

G. B. Kelly appears to hit near the mark on egoism versus altruism. Both are facts, but the completely self-conscious egoist
becomes such only at the end of a process, and after that he
owns and enjoys his own powers so completely that he will
not permit an idea to become his master. Such egoism pro-
duces acts which the altruist may mistake for altruistic acts,
but the self-conscious egoist treats ideas as his property, takes
them apart and examines them at his pleasure, and sees that
they serve his purpose and do not make him their servant.
The child is physically dependent. The youth becomes subject to the power of ideas. Pre-Christian society, wrestling with
physical powers, corresponds to childhood in the individual.
Christianity, rationalism, humanitarianism, communism, moralism,—idealism, in a word,—correspond to the enthusiastic
dreams of youth. In that stage egoism is scorned, though it
persists without general acknowledgment except as alleged
baseness. To the humanitarian idealist it is the substitute for
Devil, as Humanity is the substitute for God. The individual
who finally becomes conscious of himself is, just as he is, a
universe, —humanity itself. He then knows that he has been
dreaming about a something which is, after all, himself. He
is incomparable. The process of thought that brings him to
recognize himself can nevermore be continued as a process
in which himself would be only a factor, for he is a greater
fact than his ideas. Henceforth ideas are simply his possession.
True views are useful, but any alleged sacred Truth is romanti-
cism, or rant. When he does an act which to others may look
unegoistic, it is nevertheless to be tested by this: Is it genuinely
the will of the doer,—his good pleasure? Then it is purely egoistic. The egoist who has become self-conscious knows what
he wills, and does just as he wills so far as he can. He interests
himself in any pursuit or neglects any without a thought that
he is fulfilling or slighting any calling or mission or duty, or
doing right or wrong. All such words are impertinent. Nothing is sacred or above him. He recognizes forces, and does the
best he can to make himself master of what he wants. The

mental processes of selfhood are not those of justifying any conduct, as with the idealist, or seeking what will conform to a standard or serve a cause; but thought becomes an instrument to determine what course will procure what is desired. Are the means the best adjustable to the end? They are adopted. Justification is a piece of superstitious nonsense. Having found the pearl of great price,— come to a recognition of self,—we never throw it away. We give away what we like to give away, because we like. We may give life itself. But to the last we do our own will. Right and wrong, crime and virtue, are simply people's ideas, of no consequence to the egoist except as such ideas make fanatics and dangerous people or make serviceable subjects. No one is a self-conscious egoist, to whom wrong in natural society means more than imprudence. The egoist, as an irrepressible, conscienceless criminal, is the coming force, who will destroy all existing institutions. Mark what is called criminal. It is always some action which is the retort to the egoistic pretension of a man or of an institution. It will make a great difference when many egoists become, fully self-conscious and not ashamed of being conscienceless egoists. Language is now Christian; so the egoist has no very appropriate means of expression. His will and pleasure is not, however, a cause, or matter to be pleaded and granted. Of course he will take unbridled Liberty. Think of our language when its common expressions are such that people are asked to assume tho propriety of men's wearing bridles! And they do wear them. A few self-conscious egoists, such as popes, kings, presidents, legislators, judges, and generals, rule the world because other people are in confusion, as unconscious egoists fearing their own nature and believing they ought to obey ideas.

TAK KAK.

Egoism in Sexual Relations.

Liberty, vol. 4 no. 6 (July 17, 1886): 5.

A proverb says: "All is fair in love and war." This is a recognition of the superior force of egoism in sexual relations. What man seeks a woman from the sentiment of duty to unite? It would be absurd. In this matter liking, inclination, guides. As in eating and drinking, equally primary needs of the individual, personal appetite and taste cannot be subordinated to a foreign standard of "right." Information, which the individual can make his own and which may aid him to choose what is best for himself, is the only pertinent influence, unless one is superstitious. Is not the disparagement of natural inclinations in sex a really striking, and to the natural man or woman a disgusting, piece of superstition? It is avowedly a disparagement of egoism, or selfhood, in one of its most powerful, irrepressible manifestations. It is by observing the play of personal inclination in such matters of primary importance that we know egoism to be the undeniable law of life.

TAK KAK.

Regicides and Republicans.

Liberty, vol. 4 no. 11 (November 20, 1886): 5.

If in Germany, for example, there were a republican movement, and there were a society preaching death to the Kaiser and his officials with the view of establishing the republic, upon an arrest and trial for any violence committed by adherents of the regicidal society would not the monarchical press and tribunals seize upon the occasion to declare that, as the regicides are republicans, the republicans are regicides and their principle is to kill officials? This may serve to show the casual relation between Anarchism and bomb-throwing.

When the Southern States seceded, the Republican party declared that Democracy means secession. When Booth, a Democrat, killed Lincoln, the Republican orators and papers declared that Democracy meant assassination, and that the Democratic party must surrender its name and organization.

Those who fancy that Anarchy is compromised by what has happened at Chicago can draw the comparison.

On the day when the news of Lincoln's death was flashed to the capital of Iowa, a Republican politician entered a room where over a dozen men were at work and exclaimed: "They have assassinated the president. Now I am in favor of hanging every copperhead!" There were two Democrats present, and one of them had nerve to reply: "You would take a pretty big contract!"

The Democratic party did not disband. Republicanism is not dead by reason of its regicides or of the regicides who are not republicans. The Irish league has not renounced its object because of the incident in Phoenix Park. Free traders are not scared into becoming protectionists because contrabandists have killed revenue officers. Free traders are not required by reason to admit that the violent smuggler is a worse or even as noxious a growth as the government which makes smuggling a crime according to statute. Neither will Anarchists be frightened out of their rational consistency by clamor arising out of conflicts between the police and enemies of the present form of government or of all government, — be the case as it may. One may will an end and yet differ widely as to the means, and different persons may resort to violence with very different purposes, or no purpose that could be classed with relation to social organization.

In scientific Anarchism method is of paramount importance. No ebullitions of passion or acts of violence can really compromise the principle. Governmentalists would certainly not admit that wars and malversation of public funds settle the question whether some sort of government is necessary and useful. If the crimes of governments do not close the discussion against government, the wildest or the most ruthless acts of alleged Anarchists could never close the discussion against Anarchism, the theory of Liberty and voluntary mutual assurance as the best substitute for government, alias rulership, alias tyranny. All the attacks of ignorant and starving men upon the police go to impeach government, as symptoms show the disease. Anarchism comes before the people as the science of living and letting live.

Tak Kak.

The Colin Campbell Suit.

Liberty, vol. 4 no. 13 (January 1, 1887): 4.

A discussion is going on about the propriety of publishing in the newspapers the reports of the Colin Campbell divorce suit, and many heads of families have expressed the opinion that the publication should not be made. For one thing, they are afraid that innocent girls will get bad ideas about married life. The report of the trial will certainly give them an idea of some of its dangers. The so-called purists do not appear to reflect upon what is the reason or cause of the publication. Here is a wife who finds her husband diseased. She tells him that she cannot consent to relations which poison her health. Under Anarchy her decision would be the law of the case. He could have no rights over her person. But under statute law this man is licensed to persecute this woman.

The statute provides for a public trial, so that a court and jury may determine whether the woman shall be again free from the disgusting individual whom she has taken for her husband without knowing of his disease. The law invites him to attempt to prove her relations with other men as a reason why she shall not go free of him! Hence the reports. They spring out of the trial. The law arranges for a public washing of dirty linen, and then the admirers of statute law are shocked at the publication of the testimony and cross-examinations, which nothing but the law has made necessary. If the so-called purists want to abolish such publications, let them abolish the laws providing for divorce suits, and substitute a simple recognition of the natural and inalienable right of every individual to govern himself or herself in sexual relations.

Tak Kak.

The Rational Utilitarian Philosophy.

Liberty, vol. 4 no. 13 (January 22, 1887): 8.

In Mr. J. F. Kelly's able article on George's "Protection or Free Trade," I perceive, as the editor of *Liberty* has justly observed, that Stirner's views and my own have been misapprehended. To us Liberty is a good in itself and the means of all other good. We study direct and also remoter results. I generalize, like Mr. Kelly; and about murder I *generalize* like Mr. Kelly.

This word murder denotes killing, but it connotes also that the killing is not approved according to a rule, law, or generalization.

As to the end justifying the means, that sentiment is foreign to my standpoint. The justification intended by theology and "humanism" is not an adjustment of means to ends, but the gaining the approval of some supernal power.

Like Stirner, I simply do my own will. I act from desire, not from awe. Those who do their own will we classify as distinct from those who act under awe and obedience to supposed moral obligations,—whether conceived as commands or the equivalent impression,—from a source outside the individual, telling him to submit himself and forego his own inclinations. Holding that awe is a pernicious influence, otherwise called religion and superstition, we hold to egoism,—defined as acting out one's self.

> To thy own self be true,
> And it must follow us the night the day
> Thou canst not then be false to any man.

I should not infer from Mr. George's words, "supporting any measure that will attain that object," that he, a rabid governmentalist, meant more than measures of legislation.

As Mr. Kelly speaks of a tendency to "disrupt society," I will note that Stirner has used the word society in such a way that the dissolution of society by individuals becoming independent has no more terrors, when understood, than Proudhon's dissolution of property,—society standing for the invasive community in all its spontaneous forms beyond the family.

TAK KAK.

Proudhon's Works a Source of Health.

Liberty, vol. 4 no. 16 (February 26, 1887): 1.

Dear Mr. Tucker:

I am glad that you nave hit upon the plan of issuing Proudhon's works in monthly parts, which will not lessen their beauty and value in volumes, Proudhon had such wonderful intelligence, coupled with such unswerving determination to reveal truth, that his writings are not only in the highest degree instructive, but refreshing and encouraging,—a source of health and gladness to all those who can read them, and are not afraid of the truth. His command of language and his scholarship fully fitted him to lead in the revolution. The defenders of organized plunder have tried to keep silence about the ideas which Proudhon has made plain, and to discuss silly Communistic schemes instead. Anybody who will advocate a government can get a hearing, and the orthodox plunderers will proceed to prove that the new scheme of government is either worse than theirs, and ought therefore to be rejected, or better than theirs, and therefore "impracticable." But when they read in Proudhon or in other works, what is simply true, and candidly stated, both the litterateur and the politician turn away, saying: "That will not do. It would overturn all institutions, and, first of all, the mention of it would ruin our position." Their position depends upon the favor of capitalists. Well, I believe that it is within the power of us laboring people — of those of us who know these things— to end this pitiful state of affairs by spreading the light. We all need Proudhon's thought, even for mental health. As one to whom both languages are familiar, I can say that your translation is admirable. You have my subscription for ten copies. I should not consider myself an Anarchist if the effective desire to buy and circulate these books did not arise in me. Those who read only English can't do without your translation. Yours cordially,

TAK KAK.

Truth and Belief

Liberty, vol. 4 no. 17 (March 12, 1887): 7.

In No. 93 of *Liberty* there occur the following words written by Miss Kelly: "When ... lapse ... the Tak Kaks into the denial of all truth and justice."

In reply to this suggestion, let me offer the following from Stirner, page 117: "If an era lies enmeshed in an error, there are always some who derive advantage from it, while the others bear the injury resulting. In the middle ages the error was universal among Christians that the Church must have supreme power on earth. The hierarch believed not less in this 'truth' than the laity, and both were stuck fast in the same error. But the hierarchs had the advantage of the power which it gave, and the laity suffered the injury of subjection. As the saying is, we learn wisdom by suffering; and so the laity at length became wise, and no longer believed in the medieval 'truth.' A similar relation occurs between the middle class and the working class. Burgher and workman believe in the 'truth' of money. Those who do not possess it believe in it not less than those who do possess it, and so the laity like the priests."

On page 40 of Stirner, read: "Why is an irrefragable mathematical truth — which, according to the usual understanding of words, might be called even an eternal one—not a sacred truth? Because it is not a revealed truth, or not the revelation of a higher being."

Following this is a clear explanation how "revelation" is not confined to theology, but the ideal and general "man" becomes the object of worship, as a higher being than the individual man, and the source of so-called truths, rights, and ideas to be held sacred.

Nobody fears that mathematical truths will not maintain themselves without help of my veneration. If even science has its intolerance, it must be that it has its hypotheses which demand devout behavior, respect, not doubt. I value all the truth I know, but I value it simply as my possession. Instead of denying it, I use it as my own. I will give at another time a few words on justice, which will be as plain.

Tak Kak.

Stirner on Justice.

Liberty, vol. 4 no. 18 (March 26, 1887): 7.

On page 79 of his book, entitled *Der Einzige und Sein Eigenthum*, Stirner speaks of the insidious revival of sacred ideas and their domination, as that men are taught to regard themselves as called to devote themselves, to renounce their own wishes in favor, for example, of family, country, science, etc., and to be faithful servants of the same. "Here," he says, "we strike the immemorial craze of the world, which has not yet learned to dismiss priestcraft. To live and to labor for an idea is proposed as the high calling of man, and according to the fidelity of its fulfillment his human worth is measured. This is the domination of the idea, or priestcraft. Robespierre, for example, and St. Just, etc., were thorough priests. Thus St. Just exclaims in a speech: 'There is something terrible in the sacred love of country. It is so exclusive that it sacrifices everything to the public interest without pity, without, fear, without human regard. It hurls Manlius over the precipice; it sacrifices private inclinations; it conducts Regulus to Carthage, casts a Roman into the chasm, and places Marat in the Pantheon as a sacrifice to his devotion.'

"A world of countless 'personal' profane interests stands opposed to these advocates of ideal or sacred interests. No idea, no system, no sacred cause is so great that it should never be outweighed and modified by these personal interests. Even if in times of rage and fanaticism they are momentarily silent, yet they soon come uppermost again by the 'sound sense of the people.' Those ideas do not completely gain the victory till, and unless, they are no longer hostile to personal interests, i. e., till, and unless, they satisfy egoism.

"The man who is crying chestnuts before my window has a personal interest in a brisk sale, and if his wife or anybody else wishes as much for him, this as well is a personal interest. If, on the other hand, a thief were to take away his basket, there would at once arise an interest of many, of the whole city, of the entire country, or, in one word, of all who abominate theft: an interest wherein the person of the chestnut-vender would be indifferent, and in its place the category of 'one who is robbed' would appear in the forefront. But here, too, it might still all be resolved into a personal interest, each participant reflecting that he must aid in the punishment of the thief because, otherwise, unpunished stealing would become general and he also would lose his possessions. There are many, however, from whom such a calculation is not to be presumed. Rather, the cry will be heard that the thief is a 'criminal.' Here we have a judgment before us, the act of the thief receiving its expression in the conception 'crime.' Now the matter presents itself in this way: If a crime should work not the slightest damage either to me or to any of those for whom I take concern, yet nevertheless I should be zealous against it. Why? Because I am enthused for morality, filled with the idea of morality. I run down what is hostile to it. . . . Here personal interest comes to an end. This particular person who has stolen the basket is quite indifferent to my person. I take an interest only in the thief, this idea, of which that person presents an example. Thief and man are in my mind irreconcilable terms, for one who is a thief is not truly man. He dishonors man, or humanity, in himself when he steals. Departing from personal concern, we glide into philanthropy, which is usually misunderstood as if it were a love toward men, to each individual, whereas it is nothing but a love of man, of the unreal conception, of the spook. The philanthropist bears in his heart, not *tous anthropous*, men, but *ton anthropon*, man. Of course he cares for each individual, but merely for the reason that he would like to see his darling ideal realized everywhere.

"Thus there is no idea here of care for me, for you, or for us. That would be personal interest and belong in the chapter of 'earthly love.' Philanthropy is a heavenly, a spiritual, a priestly love. Man must be established in us, though we poor devils be brought to destruction in the process. It is the same priestly principle as that famous *fiat justitia, pereat mundus*. Man and justice are ideas, phantoms, for love of which everything is sacrificed: therefore the priestly minds are the ones that do sacrifice. . . .

"The most multiform things can belong and be accounted to man. Is his chief requisite deemed to be piety, religious priestcraft arises. Is it conceived to lie in morality, the priestcraft of morals raises its head. Hence the priestly minds of our time want to make a religion of everything; a religion of freedom, religion of equality, etc., and they make of every idea a 'sacred cause,' for instance, even citizenship, politics, publicity, freedom of the press, the jury, etc.

"In this sense what is the meaning of unselfishness? To have only an ideal interest, in face of which no consideration for the person counts anything!

"The hard-headed worldly man resists this, but still, for thousands' of years, he has always so far succumbed that he must bend his stiff neck and 'revere the higher power.' Priest-craft repressed him. When the worldly egoist had shaken off one higher power, — for example, the Old Testament law, the Pope of Rome, etc., — a seven-fold higher one was presently over him, for example, belief in place of the law; the transformation of all laymen into clergy, instead of a special clerical order, etc. It has been with him as with the man possessed of a devil from whom he no sooner thought himself free than seven devils entered into him."

In the foregoing extract it will be seen that the author puts himself in the place of the average man at the point where the generalization "crime" becomes a snare for the multitude. I offer this fragment as an egoistic contribution to that justice which remains to be constituted.

TAK KAK.

Egoism.

Liberty, vol. 4 no. 19 (April 9, 1887): 5-7.

I thank John F. Kelly for his labor and thought on "Morality and its Origin." His first paragraph contains two good Egoistic expressions. He is saying and doing of his own desire what some would persuade us not to expect except from a sense of obligation or duty.

To my understanding there is no inconsistency in my articles. Language is algebraical, and ideas of right can be resolved into ideas of power, capacity, and need, and these into the things in which, for the process of reasoning, power is assumed to inhere. It is noticeable that among the people the idea of right is giving place to that of ability. I am glad Mr. Kelly has seen Stirner's book. If he has read it very carefully and with perfectly open mind, I wonder that he still requires any definition of Egoism. If Stirner said hard things of right and truth, he also said that man is a phantom. This should challenge careful reading. Egoism deals with facts, breaks and dissolves the dominion of ideas, and does not propose to reestablish it in definitions and doctrines. Things can be perceived and named; motives, actions, and consequences appreciated and described. Observe in the following quotation how Stirner uses the word truth in its real sense:

The discoverer of a great truth well knows that it may be useful to other men, and, as a greedy withholding would bring him no enjoyment, he communicates it.—Der Einzige und sein Eigentum, p. 136.

Here I may introduce a sentence from page 130 on progress:

The men of future generations will yet win many a Liberty of which we do not even feel the want.

Certainly the abstract idea of right is in opposition to that of might. Force is real and, in many forms, independent of sensation and sentiment. Therefore it is said that might transcends right. A declaration of rights is often the pitiful expression of a lack of power. Just now a report says that a speaker at Chicago declared they had a right to overthrow society by force. I call that idea a foolish phantasy, the abstract, fixed, fanatical idea of right severed from circumstances which determine abilities. The devotee of the fixed idea is mad. He either runs amuck, or cowers as mesmerized by the idea. The New York "Standard" says of the rich: "It is no excuse for them that the poor would do the same thing." Say rather it is only an excuse. Moralists labor in long discussions of such excuses. Egoism would render such excuses impotent and such a line of discussion unnecessary. M. Harman of Kansas has suggested going on unoccupied land and fighting it out there, because the abstract right appears, though the fight would be a losing one: idiocy produced by the fixation of the idea, or a foolish phantasy. The same remark for the "Truth Seeker's" suggestion to Henry Appleton that, if one objects to taxation, one "ought" not to walk on pavement laid with means derived from taxation. The same for punctilios about oath-taking, about telling the truth under all circumstances, about keeping promises because they are promises, — a weakness which delays the dissipation of that intrusive despotism which alone desires to fortify itself by exacting promises. By action showing quiet contempt for undesired fancied duties to ideas and "principles," the principal himself, Ego, reduces bigotry and all tyranny to despair, and compels the importunate to desist from what they soon discover to be useless. Egoism has many practical suggestions for people in business, love, and other relations, and especially for the Anarchistic propaganda.

The intellect which has physical forces at command sometimes crushes the idealist; then what becomes of the ideas which were in his brain? The utilitarian definition of right has its meaning in that course of conduct which a utilitarian association finds desirable for itself; but, when an individual attempts to judge what is best for everybody, he is apt to make mistakes, and when he sacrifices his own welfare to an idea of the general welfare, he may see shrewder individuals profiting by his error; and, though the moralist may pronounce his conduct admirable, the result is not happy. Egoism helps the utilitarians and all others to comprehend the logic of the existence of bodies. Each body makes its declarations of what it wants as if it were an Ego. If the persons composing it are not real Egos, they will probably take the reason of the association for their reason and sacrifice themselves in circumstances where conditions are not reciprocal, or as assumed in the theory. But the real Ego has a sure rule in himself for himself. Each person is a fact.

The man who wrings from another the fruit of his labor excites me to hostility by this wringing, or wrong, because I will not suffer it if I can help it; but my suffering is not a contest between a moral principle and my own self, but the result of an offence to myself, an obstacle to the realization of my desire.

A theologian, a moralist, and myself condemn rape, and will try to prevent it. The first says that he bases his action upon the law of God, which he obeys. The second says that he bases his action upon a moral law, which he obeys. These are ideas of duty. The theologian cannot conceive that he would be moved to prevention without the law of God; hence he distrusts the moralist as having only a shadowy sanction to control him. The moralist smiles contemptuously at the obtuseness of the theologian, but suffers from his bigotry. Then the moralist turns upon me and treats me as the theologian treated him. My natural inclinations are "not sufficient restraint," he thinks, and so forth, and not sufficient incitement to do well. But really I am well, when I am whole, and holiness is but a fantastic image, made by ignorance, of wholeness. And when I am well, I shall want to do well. The first two may preach duty to the rapist! Suppose they succeed in restraining him by that influence. It must be so powerful, if it overcomes his will, as to make him subject to indoctrination in general. If to the views of the theologian, then he is ready for religious fanaticism, and — misery of parodies — the very same authority will teach him, now subject to its doctrines, that with religious sanction he may bind a woman to himself in marriage and commit rape upon her person as often as he likes. Moralism offers no better "guarantee," none whatever in fact. To dominate and control the man it must have an influence over him which, after restraining him from committing the offence in question, will fit him to commit any offence against persons when the moral idea, the greatest good of humanity, dictates it. Filled with the idea that he is a vessel of humanity devoted to the welfare of the "social organism," what guarantee is there that he will not become the instrument of Huxley in extirpatating Anarchists as carbuncles upon the said organism? What guarantee can there be that the moralized rapist will not, by force of the very idea to which he surrendered, — the idea, namely, of duty to the social organism, — become persuaded that the social organism needs scientific culture at the root as well as the pruning already mentioned, and that consequently in the cause of humanitarian science it may become his duty to commit a number of scientific rapes upon a number of women, whose Egoism, however, is detestably refractory to the sacrifice demanded by the general welfare. The dog returns to his vomit. My simple Egoism may not furnish abstruse arguments against rape, but it will not furnish the respect which now maintains rape as the recognized method of propagation and would render my life a forfeit if I followed my native impulse and slew a dozen rapists a day. But they believe that they are doing right. It is the general welfare which overrides the welfare of the individual woman.

I think the world is well stocked with sympathy. I see much expense at funerals; a wonderful amount of patriotism, ready to war for fixed ideas; the Red Cross society is liberally supported; even money-lenders are sincerely quick to relieve their victims; and an anaesthetic bullet has been invented.

As for men, or men, animals, and plants, being an organism, I do not need to discuss that. I should have to inquire as to the specific and individual characteristics of the organism. The idea is doubtless a relief from the mechanical idea of political institutions. We have the phenomena of life before us, and can judge of them as they present themselves. If I am a molecule or anything else in an organism, that is all right. I am what I am. And if old theology was a reflection of man, then surely Egoism is the fulfillment of the world's travail, for God is pictured as acting spontaneously, without a thought of duty, or pressure against his inclinations, and yet the source of all good. But if it is suggested by the moralist that I shall waive anything upon being convicted of being part of an organism, my stubborn personality may defeat the scheme, as Egoistic anti-prohibitionists defeat prohibitory laws which lack only the consent of victims. I shall not waive anything, and yet I shall be as serene and content to be a molecule, if I am one, as to be anything else, even a grain of iron tonic for the organism, or the grain of strychnine that sends it to kingdom come, or a flea upon a dog (the flea and the dog being parts of the same organism?)

Mr. Kelly's sketch of morals does not effectively antagonize Egoism, because sympathy for persons is Egoistic when it is natural. I do not attack that feeling as superstitious, and I do not attack any feeling upon the ground that the person cannot account for it. I attack as superstitious what is called moral obligation, the oppressive sense of duty, a trace of which is conveyed in Mr. Kelly's words, "this feeling that one should so act." Genuine personal sympathy is spontaneous. It is possible that Mr. Kelly's is wholly so. In places he writes somewhat like an Egoist of fine sentiment, but his entire misapprehension about Egoism, as repeatedly explained, goes further than his particular use of the words "should" and "ought" and his talk about morality to show that he cannot be an Egoist. For, had he been an Egoist, he would have "caught on" to some of the numerous statements by Stirner or myself which would show him that Egoism, or selfhood, has nothing in the world to do with broad or narrow caricatures upon it. If a man is small or large in capacity or range of capacities, yet if he owns himself and is awed by no command, bewitched by no fixed idea or superstition, but does everything with a sense that his acts are his own genuine, personal, sovereign choice,— under whatever pressure of material circumstances and necessary yielding thereto, —then the man is an Egoist, or one conscious that he is a genuine Ego, an individual, a free man according substantially to Proudhon's definition of a free man, printed as a motto in *Liberty* last year. If the moralists, like the theological religionists, are so sceptical about

personal character as to have no confidence in its producing good behavior, the Egoist will only say this,—that he discovers in himself nothing which he can call moral obligation. You may therefore observe his acts if you care to do so, and perhaps you will discover that what you vainly attributed t o the restraint of moral obligation is the spontaneous nature of yourself, but debased with the alloy of scepticism as to your own personal character. In this view, what becomes of the proposed just mean between Egoism and Altruism? It is, of course, the result of a ridiculous perversion of terms. In the first place Egoism was degraded together with human nature, its subject, to the greater glory of God. Then, Egoism having been assigned the popular meaning which implies that a man without an infusion of divine grace or moral efficacy will simply grub to satisfy hunger and vanity, Altruism was invented to mean doing acts to benefit others. There are no Egoists who do not do many acts to help others. Generosity is perfectly Egoistic. There is no quality so distinctively so, in contrast with dutiful moralism. is a flower of character, without the slightest taint or smut of moral polico forces in the forum of consciousness. Popular instinct and common sense recognize this fact even in the narrowest phase of individuality, — egotism. People flatter a man's vanity, — i. e., rouse his self-appreciation,—when they want to profit by his generosity. Vanity is a mortal foe to reverence.

The Egoist acts to gratify himself and not from a foreign motive. But are all acts Egoistic? All acts of unadulterated Egos are so. We cannot ignore the plain fact that men succumb to the domination of ideas. They are from infancy taught to believe and to practise and obey, and to regard Egoism as the worst of all faults, and reverence, dutifulness toward something or other, as necessary; some standard outside of their own tastes and desires as authoritative and guiding; some things as sacred, not to be touched or brought into question. This is religion, and, as diluted, moral obligation; and it is so proved by the dread that everything will go wrong if men have only their own desires and intelligence as factors determining their conduct, or Liberty and intelligence, as Proudhon has defined them. We call the anti-Egoistic influence fixed ideas, or spiritual domination. We say that we will possess ideas, but they shall not possess us. But for the surrender to fixed ideas and the drilling and teaching which maintain their dominion, the State and the Church would be only so many men, their sacredness gone. How long would their power endure against the surprise, ridicule, indifference, or aversion of a mass of Egoists? Superstition is a plant which grows from any bit of root left in the ground. If there is a single thing in which the individual shrinks from pursuing that in which he is most interested, or if he submits to control by ideas which have not come in the way that makes them part of himself, he is undone, precisely as, if any branch of government is established, it may bring back the whole apparatus of despotism. Freethinkers as to theology have changed.masters when they have become moralists or remained patriots. Charles Bradlaugh wrote in his paper that the shores of England seemed to him more sacred than any others. To the Egoist there is nothing sacred. But, when Bradlaugh took an oath, and stated that his views were too well known for there to be any misunderstanding about it, he was in line with the Egoistic method of reducing bigotry: teaching the bigots that cobwebs do not bind real persons.

The secularists had their chance when their term was new, and they started officially non-political and with an intention to treat theology simply as a topic for individual expressions. Secularism itself was put forward as holding nothing sacred. But in a short time its founder, G. J. Holyoake, recanted by declaring that the secular is sacred in its influence on life and character. After that it could not be Egoistic, and for want of Egoistic affirmation it missed advancing to Anarchism, and reverted to an anti-theological protest,— the old formula of wailing "rights of conscience."

To those who believe that Liberty will produce a better order than authority I would suggest a reconsideration if they have condemned Egoism. It is certain that whatever gets to the form of desire must be gratified or repressed. The habit of repressing certain desires for personal motives, wisdom, will be much more valuable to the individual than the habit of repressing them from a sense of cosmic duty. Whoever has outgrown that enslaving idea and found that the sun is not blotted out of his sky has gained an experience which he would not relinquish for all the treasures of other men. Egoism is the solid base of Anarchism and of atheism. Though it does not necessarily render each Egoist agreeable to all other Egoists, it destroys the awe, reverence, and obedience upon which all despotisms thrive.

It is difficult to imagine all men as knowing what are the needs of all other men in taste and sympathy. It is less difficult to imagine all men as having become Egoists. Then, with the general diffusion of economic science rendering any overreaching conduct impossible in either case, Egoism seems to offer the advantage that it affords no leverage for any disposition which may arise to meddle with or exploit tastes and sympathies; while it utterly extirpates the moral craze or fanatical motive.

Let us suppose all men Egoists. How would the pope persuade people to support him? How would Bismarck persuade Germans that they have &h individual interest in holding Alsace? How would Lord Salisbury persuade Englishmen that they have an interest in holding Ireland? How would Grover Cleveland persuade us to support him and coerce the Mormons? Yet natural sympathy would give all the aid required by any Mormon woman who wanted to leave her husband. In fact, if she were an Egoist, she could be restrained only by physical force; but we know that neither compulsion nor any indoctrination in moral duty is necessary to cause natural affection. Egoism therefore points to a general letting alone, and to the consequent growth of people fitted by environment to live and let live. In this light the ridiculous dispute as to whether duality or variety in love is the better plan is simply referred to natural inclinations. The fittest will survive: an axiom which bespeaks the supremacy of material conditions, unconscious forces in part and other forces of which there is no consciousness in me. It means that that will survive which can survive. It does not mean that that which is judged most moral will survive. A hardy negro sailor would survive where Herbert Spencer would be drowned. The Egoists will survive in the long run, as they carry no useless baggage and keep their eyes open. They seek to disprove all things which they are able to disprove by scrutiny and shaking, and consequently they get rid of those unsound combinations among which unsound men are trying to survive. By getting at the unshakable for conditions the Egoist will attain the greatest simplicity of formula and the most solid basis for himself to be a survivor. Fittest for what? and how fit? For survival, and by ability to survive. The hyena steak the babe. The fittest (subject) survives (predicate); or the survivor (subject) is called the fittest (predicate) without other idea or evidence of fitness. The ideal is that which is desired. Moralists ignore the potency of things in relation to produce desired results by generating personal desire to the point of efficient action.

The manners that best serve men, from any point of view, can be determined only according to the character of the men concerned. For equitable commerce I need men of understanding and purpose, and first of all I need real men. Then I can hope that economic science will be appreciated. As for the Egoists who prey upon the masses, they do so because the masses are exploitable material, easily beguiled, filled with spiritual ideas, and entertained with moral doctrines.

The spiritual man is mad. We can do nothing with men who are not substantially whole men. Mr. Kelly's idea that "society" may be diseased suggests for me the analogy of minds diseased. At least they are perverted, stuffed with bigotry, and notions of fate, charms, luck, national glory, party, duty, self-sacrifice, belief in their own tendency to wickedness, therefore of the need of restraint. They are indoctrinated, not educated; taught to believe and to distrust their own nature even by moralists who do not suspect that moralism is in degree the same scepticism as religious faith. For education we need to begin with this: Be yourself. I affirm, not as a reason, but as a result, behavior satisfactory to others in a greater degree than from any moral system. I affirm that selfhood is the law of nature (to use a convenient expression generalizing facts, not meaning a law to be obeyed) and that minds are poisoned, debauched, deflected, and subjugated, that men are rendered insane, when they give their consent to place their mental centre of gravity outside of themselves; then they are not genuine individuals. The attraction of the outer world is for the Ego as a complete person acting without sense of pressure or dictation. For results, if you say that some Egos are narrow and "selfish," I say I prefer them as narrow Egos rather than take the chances of what may happen should they acquire a "sense of duty'" and become patriots, moralists, or exponents of any fixed idea whatever. Egoism is sanity. Non-Egoism is insanity.

Egoistic interest includes "all that may become a man." Egoistic prudence is calculation as to the means of satisfying a desire or avoiding an undesired issue. It regards the good of another when I really desire that good. I watch the rising of good-will in myself and permit no idea to become my master. Ideas are my furniture, my possession. Feelings shall not be imparted to me; but they may be aroused. Egoistic self-denial will now be clear. Egoistic beneficence exists now. Egoistic justice and practical duty will be constituted in and by the presence of Egos and their mutual requirements. In dealing with insane people we cannot do any other justice than to do the best we can. The Ego who does not feel any sentiment for company can "flock by himself," but. when dealing with other Egos, he will find an adjustment established in all transactions upon the basis of the utter impossibility of any one who may be deficient as compared with others in sentiment, getting what he does not earn.

What boots it to preach ideas of Right and Wrong as motives? If you find believers, they are stuffed with your idea, and have no root in themselves. But if you dispel fixed ideas and cultivate persons, you will have the sentiments and actions natural to real and unadulterated persons. There may be much seeming self-sacrifice, but, if it is made with pleasure, it is not self-sacrifice. If it is not made with personal satisfaction, it is insanity; it is real self-sacrifice. There is no just mean about the matter. If there is an exact relation between myself and the rest of men, it will, I am sure, find its solution in my acting as a sovereign individual. I shall discover whether they are such or not, and treat them accordingly. But thus I act at all events, and kindly to the weak. Let nature use me, if she will and can; I can at least say that she shall use me only on condition that her organic purposes are effected by organic processes, and that my conscious will and satisfaction is the stamp of genuineness upon her processes so far as I am concerned. Digestion and assimilation, please: no hypodermic injections of spiritual powers. What is that power which would conscript me, or come in, not at the door, hut another way, climbing over the wall? It is a thief and a robber.

If without restraint I am dangerous in act, then put physical restraint upon me. That is your affair. If murder is the tendency of a mind unawed, the social sanction will want an ecclesiastical despotism. If conscience means simply sentiment, not the conscience which does make cowards of all victims of spiritual hallucinations, I have nothing here to say of conscience. The tendency to murder is commonly asserted against Anarchy by all advocates of government. We reply as Anarchists that governments murder their millions, and so the dozen murders which might occur under Anarchism in a year would not seem to be much of an argument. I 'can leave the matter there in the same terms for Egoism, substituting spiritual ideas—i. e., fixed ideas — for government. And as government reposes upon the fixity of idea of the people regarding the need of government, it is essentially ,dependent upon the continuance of the fixed idea. Egoism dissolves, not one fixed idea merely, but the habit and faith of fixity, therefore all, and furnishes the condition for the final eradication of all political domination; for it will not be thought that a dominion of military power would be possible without a glamour of belief or fixed idea in the people. So long, however, as moralists have influence to persuade men that they cannot and ought not to trust themselves as natural sovereigns obeying only the promptings of their own instincts, judgment, and natural sentiments, they will persuade them to a habit of deferring to doctrines of right and wrong, ideal, fantastic, utterly subversive of spontaneous action, and tending to continue and renew the influence of teachers and expounders; and these will have opportunity to build up hierarchies and governments. The treacherous enemy in the citadel is the fixed idea. Until the fixity is dissolved, the victim will demand only reforms and obtain only changes of masters.

Of course selfhood asserts itself against the physical tyranny of other persons, whether singly or aggregated, in family, tribe, clan, nation; but self-ownership, so far as outward appearances are concerned, is largely admitted, and would follow as a result, if subjection were not secured by means of ideas. The power of the government to collect taxes; that of landlords to collect rent and hold open land, — would be exhausted and would utterly fail if it had not consent in the victims generally either directly to these exactions or to the system of which they are parts. We take Liberty when we no longer feel bound. The bondage of idea is now the great bondage. In matters already viewed Egoistically, such as drinking, sexual intercourse, gain, authority is practically defeated. Authority, whether of Egoists or fanatics, can be overthrown only by Egoism. The harlot, the gambler, the usurer, the libertine, persist in their individual course because they are not amenable to authoritative control except by actual, constant watching, and this would be too expensive. Their example teaches passive resistance, but passive resistance can come only when, as in these cases, the idea of duty to obey is removed. Egoism dispels it altogether, and exhibits the reality, Ego. Religion and moralism say that we may have passions, but we must not allow our passions to enslave us. The Egoist extends the suggestion to include ideas. He has ideas, but he remains the master of them, fully aware that any of them might grow upon him and enslave him, if permitted, such is the tendency to give to airy nothings a local habitation and fortify it against its owner Moralism may say we ought to be free because that is best for the totality. The Egoist says, to himself at least, "I am the master of myself." Then he acts of course according to his natural character under the circumstances in which he may be placed. The Egoist cannot be bound, except in physical bonds, because there are no others. With the moralist, the stone is around the fruit to hold it in. With the Egoist, all the precious thoughts which are supposed by the moralists to create obligations are possessions which create desires; and personality cannot lead to all sorts of contradictory desires. No moral law is needed to prevent a nightingale from adopting the habits of a raven. The Egoist realizes that he is truly an animal, and that ideas have just as much existence as language, no more, — that is, they are processes. All the ideas he has he will use as he sees fit. If of a speculative intellectual turn, the Egoist cannot doubt that there is the greatest good for all in Egoism, and, as he can find satisfaction in proving it, he may undertake to do so.

Anarchism is the direct outgrowth of the natural fact of Egoism directed against the visible enemy sustained upon the weakness of invaded and debauched personality. The new creation, in effect, is a banishment of unreal fascinations. Let there be men, and there are men, whole men.

TAK KAK.

Reply to John F. Kelly.

Liberty, vol. 4 no. 24 (July 2, 1887): 7.

Mr. Kelly asks what is there superstitious in respect for the
rights of others? That depends on what is meant. Stirner uses
the verb "to respect" in the sense of to stand In awe, and this
not with reference to physical force. When desire and " sacred
duty " coincide, there is no test presented.

I use the word egoism in only one general meaning, defined in No. 97. When the symbol is understood, accepted, and
its meaning remembered, there is no difficulty in applying it,
however many different manifestations there may be of the
Ego. Vanity, which prompts men to say I—I—I, is popularly
called egotism. It is a particular manifestation of the Ego. I
recognize the fact that vanity is Egoistic and turned this to
account to exhibit an "altruistic" benefit, but possibly cozening.
One could raise trifling criticisms on the difference between an
"altruistic" benefit intended for some others and such a benefit
for all others. Eccentricity is individual, but the fact does not
destroy the proper general meaning of individuality. Having
already defined my principal term, what more is expected of
me in that relation? To define popular variations indicating
special developments? In such cases it surely suffices that the
special meaning be made clear then and there, which was the
case when alluding to vanity and introducing the popular term
egotism so as not to falsify the popular spelling and at the same
time not to convey the idea that vanity is the whole of Egoism.
Men have different tastes and appetites. In gratifying any of
them they exhibit Egoism. That is the reason why there are so
many different kinds of the article.

Has it dawned upon Mr. Kelly that Egoism is perhaps not
a bad word in itself, and that it might be stigmatizing personality to use it to designate merely repulsive traits of character?
But will a " t " save the mark or drive philosophers to a hyphen1

I shall not object to a good thing for its name, even if I object to the name, and though evolutionary moralism puts out
its head when it hears the hind part of its name. When unen-
lightened people have done harm, we will inquire what caused
them to do harm. We need not disturb the "chestnut" style of

religious controversy. The greatest reason why a particular Ego will not rob his neighbor may be that he does not want to do so. Why might not Mr. Kelly tell the readers of *Liberty* what Stirner said in reproach to the thief?

Bismarck must go with the Pope. Emperor Wilhelm and Vaterland are to him indispensable superstitions.

There is just this about all motives being Egoistic (it is like chemical substances being physical), —that for it to be a true statement the word "motive" must be restricted to a meaning which renders the proposition tautological. If a motive is a calculation with personal desire at the end, then only in the degree in which one is a real Ego can one entertain a motive. The hypnotized subject is otherwise moved, and not as a self-governing person; though we speak of him as a person, as we speak of a dead duck as a duck.

If promises disappeared, Mr. Kelly thinks that contracts and concerted action would become impossible except under duress, but I think that contracts will have to become mutually beneficial with appreciable continuity, and by beneficial I mean as well gratifying to the sentiments as to what are popularly appreciated as the material interests of the contracting parties. Every reasonable man knows that, when an arrangement is satisfactory to him, he will not break it up merely because the contract has expired. Even those who believe in the sacredness of promises and contract will admit as much.

I have yet to find the moralist who treats a promise as a law of nature, admitting of no exception, and so with always telling the truth, as when one is in the power of an enemy. The moralist has his superior reason. I have mine. To me a promise contains two elements, —namely, (1) the announcement of a purpose, and (2) respect for the "sacredness" of the engagement. The Egoist will either construe promise as an announcement, or will substitute the less misleading simple announcement. One who withdraws from his announced purpose, to our injury, must furnish reasons satisfactory to us or expect us to mark his conduct and deal with him as wavering or hostile.

It is really curious to read that, if pledges are valueless, "his colleagues would sell him out on the first opportunity." Does a natural man refrain from selling out his friends only because he has given a pledge not to do so? If so, it is much to be feared that he will sell them out in any event at the first good chance. The greatest traitor gives the most solemn assurances and invents the longest and strongest oaths Better than all such vanities, follies, and credulities is this: Those who are against us must expect us to be against them, and those who do not love our way we do not want.

The Einzige is Stirner's term for the genuine Ego. Napoleon was not altogether such, but how much he lacked is immaterial to my reply. He had a number of propensities which certainly could not be argued away. Whatever he was, he was taken as an idol, deified and served by the unegoistic devotion of others who did the slaughtering and pillaging. To accomplish all this mischief it was necessary that there be national spirit and a variety of other bate-breeding superstitions, not only in France, but in the antagonistic countries.

Men have interests in each other prior to contract. Neither is the moralism which makes a promise sacred nor coercion in an Archistic sense necessary to contract. They can boycott the recalcitrant. The Ego is not a spook, but an animal. I have not attempted to prove Mr. Kelly superstitious because he retains the terms "ought" and "should." If the reader will refer to No. 97, where I alluded to Mr. Kelly's "particular use" of those terms, — not to the fact of his using them,—he will see the nature of Mr. Kelly's error on this point, which is surprising. And really Mr. Kelly, having formerly written on moral obligation, now takes a singular course in confining his gratuitous instances of the word "ought" to indications of probabilities, as How much ought this to measure, etc. If these illustrations illustrate adequately, one might infer that, when the moralist asks, How ought a man to act in certain circumstances? he only means how will he act? I use the same words myself not only to indicate probabilities, but also to indicate conduct which I will approve or disapprove for various reasons. A whist player ought not to trump his partner's ace. I ought not to write on both sides of this paper. An Anarchist ought not to vote. I ought to answer candidly, if at all. In each instance it is implied that the Ego has given himself a certain task, or has a certain purpose, and that something conditions its fulfillment.

My liking will determine whether I play whist or not, whether I write or not. My dislike of tyranny will determine me, with information, to be a plumb-liner.

Curious reasoning is this: "It seems as if Tak Kak had so recently succeeded in getting rid of some of his incubi that," etc. "Of course he can scarcely be expected to grasp the idea, then, that," etc. I draw attention to the connective "then." The premise which is conditioned by "it seems," leads to a conclusion which is obviously Mr. Kelly's basis for asserting that "it seems." Because I "fail to grasp," I "seem " green, and because I am green, inasmuch as I seem to be green, I " fail to grasp." Perhaps I have given enough thought to the question to hold up my end. Is Mr. Kelly confident that I am very green? What length of time appears to him sufficient for self-examination? I am glad that the organ of the plumb-liners is liberal enough to let this discussion in even for amusement. Readers need a little entertainment.

Bradlaugh's perjury could have no interest for me except as illustrating the principle upon which tyranny, relative or absolute, may be combatted, just as I spoke of passive resistance by gamblers.

The sense of honor which "gratifies" Mr. Kelly is by that word indicated to be Egoistic. If Mr. K. were one of those men who bend in pain and agony to gratify a tyrannous sentiment of honor, the aspect would be different. Adulterated sugar is called sugar, and adulterated, warped Egos are called persons "obedient to a sense of honor and duty."

If Mr. Kelly is not a "good citizen" or not a "cooperator," but simply a good resident and an advocate of equity in individual relations as resulting in something better than cooperative organizations, he will be denounced by those to whom not to be a "good citizen" is to be a bad man, and to whom not to vote is not to be a good citizen. Words in their primary and even secondary meanings tempt to acceptance, but often betray us in their further connotations or technical meanings. The secondary meaning of the word morals may be approved conduct, but under the head of secondary Mr. Kelly has introduced a distinction which may be referred to a third stage. When Belford Bax and B. R. Tucker speak of the inexpedient, they plainly mean that which they deem a mistake in judgment. When they speak of the immoral, they appear to mean that which they will condemn as to its temper or purpose. If the word morality might stand for the words good conduct, and immorality for the words bad conduct, then it would be equally open to all to use them judiciously with reference to any conceived good or bad, for an individual or group. But moralism as distinguishing itself from Egoism demands more. It will have morality to be the "truly" good conduct, and, if an individual is so organized that what is for his good is not for the good of the supreme spook of morality, he is not allowed in thought to be a standard of good for himself. Thus the moralists are impelled by the specific character of their idea to become dogmatic. Compare what I suggest as the real secondary meaning of the word "morals" with the common use of the word murder; for what is true of moralism is true of particular words indicating moral acts. The Egoist may talk of temperance, duty, obligation, right, or anything else relating to conduct, but be will always intend to convey his individual judgment, and with reference to his own line of conduct, never to make himself the mouthpiece of a dogma. When the Czar kills a Nihilist, he calls it an execution, but the Nihilists call it a murder. When the Nihilists kill a Czar, they call it an execution, but the Czarites call it murder. Still, though every one puts his own judgment into words which express the several parts of morals, the distinctive moralists are not content to leave the word morality in the same elective state.

For further illustration, there is Mr. Tucker's use of the word right in the article alluded to. As we give each other rights and give ourselves duties, when one says that a man has a right to do such and such a thing, I know that, whatever else he may mean-, he means that it will be right so far as he is concerned. He is willing to let the man do that. Note the contrast with the course of certain men who have urged others to do unwise acts because the theoretical right appeared:

To restrain some men by preaching devotion to the spook of moralism may be quite possible. The moralist makes an easy case thus, like the other religionists; nevertheless I distrust moralism. It draws comparisons between the actual and its

42

ideal without well considering what can be realized and how. Drunkenness is immoral. Preach the welfare of the social life. Magnetize the drunkard. Still there is something in his stomach which moralism does not reach. What other evil will appear I do not know. Perhaps moralism preserves him to beget a race of drunkards or fanatics.

The perpetuation of the social life is a phrase in which the spook nests. After preaching, each person will translate it for himself and have his separate spook. Is society all living persons, or also all persons who are to live? The moralist may think of his children as contributing to form the ideal "society" which he carries in his head. If they die before maturity, "society" never is what he thought of. It does not include those persons whom he imagined as his grandchildren.

Are animals excluded from "the social life " simply in the degree of their inability to enter? If the answer is Yes, then moralism is a fiction. If the answer is No, then "moral" society is an arbitrary selection,—a characterization of and for themselves by a set of bipeds who have seized all advantages over less intelligent animals. The horse has feelings, but not such capacities as to render him the equal of the man. Now, if moralism fully respects life and feeling and happiness as such, the moral society will let the wild horse alone; but if the bipeds capture the quadruped, castrate him, make him a beast of burden and keep him in slavery, — ab, the unconscious hypocrisy! If, however, the moralist is determined to maintain moralism as his superior principle, he must respect the animals whose Inability alone debars them from society. Let him kill the wolf in self-defence, but let him not kill the wolf because it kills the lamb, and then himself kill the lamb and eat it. It is not necessary that he take a horse to ride, or to draw a carriage. He can walk and carry burdens. Let the moralist set this example, or cease to preach moralism as a principle of disinterested respect for life and feeling as such. But what is there in a man that distinguishes him, except in degree, from other animals? The older moralists had a ready reply. They respected the immortal soul. If moralism is to be commended because Mr. Kelly can influence somebody, will he not bethink himself that the doctrine of an immortal soul in the negro had something to do with setting negroes free? It is the Egoist's turn to laugh if the moralist finds that other ideas which are not true may have served to promote some good at times.

It is Egoistic to select for aid those who can and will aid us. Proudhon did not contemplate that we must give ourselves duties to all men without regard to their ability or willingness to be of us, with us, and for us. He was not one inch removed from Stirner in his view when he spoke of giving a youth a chance to show himself, and then, if he did not defend himself against oppression: "Frappez, ce n'est pas un homme." (Strike, he is no man !)

I might further object to the term morality because it conveys the ideas of people who would interfere to repress vice, as well as the different ideas of Mr. Kelly's school. If Egoism is reproached for an appearance of like confusion in popular estimation, there are these differences,—that the various phases of Egoism are Egoism, but the so-called popular morality is to Mr. Kelly's school immoral; and also that Egoism does not pretend to make any rule at all analogous to morality. What the social welfare is must always be an individual opinion. What the pleasure of the individual is is a fact ascertainable by the individual, if anything is.

The hero-worshipper preaches duty. What would strong men and governments be without dutiful worshippers in the mass of mankind?

Tak Kak.

On Mr. Kelly's Final Statement.

Liberty, vol. 5 no. 1 (August 13, 1887): 5.

To the Editor of *Liberty* :

I think I never forgot that Mr. Kelly believes in duties prior to promises and consequently independent of promises. Against Mr. Kelly's statement that I construed him to mean that without promises we are without obligations, I refer to what has been printed. It will show that I kept Mr. Kelly's position in view, but I contended that satisfactory conduct may result from natural good will without any feeling of moral obligation.

Moral obligation is not properly denned by explaining the single word " obligation " in the sense of philosophical necessity. For illustration, the embezzler and the assassin act in accordance with philosophical necessity. If Mr. Kelly should say that they act according to moral obligation, he would stultify himself.

I have never advocated killing the Chinese. In approaching other men, I am disposed to take the first steps at my own cost to see whether it is possible to derive mutual benefit from the relation.

Economics I regard as different from morals, and in economics I agree with Mr. Kelly.

By using the word "special" he has suggested something general, but this is not the way to prove that the basis of accord is anything more than similarity of organisms and conditions. One contract may be more special than another, but, to my thinking, a contract presumes simply contracting parties and conditions.

According to evolution and observation objective realities are changing. Then practical justice must take form according to the number and qualities of the objective realities which give rise to it at any time. I design writing a brief analysis of justice to show that this ideal is a composition of apperception and sympathy.

Mr. Kelly says that he knows of "no ego other than the combined ideas and feelings at any given time." Do the readers imagine, then, that Mr. Kelly has been discussing Egoism as advanced by Stirner and myself? Mr. Kelly's ego is utterly un-like our Ego. When Mr. Kelly wrote before about a spookish, unconditioned ego, I simply answered that the ego of which I speak is an animal. If there is one distinction which must be clearer than another, it is the distinction between the real and the ideal. The Ego of which I speak is real. I mean my own organism. Hence, as I speak

of the real, I can consistently speak of ideas as its furniture. But an Ego, or person, composed of ideas and feelings, would be mere moonshine. In " Der Einzige " Stirner says that he does not mean Fichte's ideal ego, but " this transitory I," the man Stirner.

In a matter of wrong (wringing, twisting) there are the doer and the sufferer, perhaps also a spectator. From their dif-ferent standpoints various considerations may arise besides that of imprudence, which latter is among the considerations specially for the wrong-doer.

Mr. Kelly has simply mistaken my meaning in the sen-tence which he correctly quotes, ending with the words " he is not allowed in thought to be a standard of good for himself." I meant in the thought of the moralist; otherwise I should have written the words in different order, with punctuation. I knew that the moralist must in fact allow me to be a standard for myself; and it would not be worth while to ask the moralist to allow me to be, in thought, a standard for myself, for over my thinking he cannot dominate. I quite agree with Mr. Kelly that, as soon as a being in pursuit of his good commits acts injurious to others, it is time for them and their allies to stop him.

I do claim and know that there is a better use for friends than to sell them; and, as I feel with Stirner, I believe that I comprehend Stirner better than Mr. Kelly does. Interest in others and profit to be derived from their company mean more to us than to the moralist, precisely as morals means more to the moralist who has rejected religion than to the religionist who regards morality as an outhouse to religion.

I have not yet undertaken to reconcile Proudhon and Stirner all the way through. For such a task the first step would be to reconcile Proudhon with Proudhon. The reasons which I and Stirner can give why the young man should be given a chance to show himself are such as I doubt not Mr. Kelly would approve. We desire to find, to aid, and be aided by as many free and intelligent men as possible. What Mr. Kelly really wants to know is how I and Stirner came to have such desires. Let him interrogate the forces which created us sentient individuals, or be content with the fact. Proudhon, who exclaimed: "A moi Lucifer, Satan, qui que tu soil, demon que lafoi de met peres opposa a Dieu et it feglise! Je porterai ta parole,"—Proudhon would not reject our aid.

The extracts given by Mr. Kelly from Proudhon show a temperament and expression very different from Stirner's. These may be found to conceal a greater degree of agreement in purpose than Mr. Kelly has yet discovered. Take these words : " And that he who has renounced God continues to adore Justice, even though it be nothing else than the commandment of himself to himself, the principle and law of social dignity." Methinks that smacks of the intrepid Stirner. Now listen to Stirner (p. 311): " It is contemptible to deceive a confidence which we have freely called forth; but it is no shame to Egoism to allow anyone who has tried to get us into his power by an oath, to suffer by the ill-success of his distrustful artifice. If you have tried to bind me learn then that I know how to break my fetters." Would this sentiment stain Proudhon ?

In the extracts it is asked, what is this Justice if not the essence that has been adored as God ? But afterward Proudhon declares war against God. May we not possibly, by a further step, have found the same essence in a still nearer form, — nothing else than the commandment of one's self to himself? If the form Justice then appears superfluous, fossilized, and an abstraction, we are advancing still to understand that of which God, and the Idea, and Rights, and Justice, were successive reflections. When I know and feel myself, I need neither God nor moral law. The Justice which Proudhon worshipped and served was an emanation from himself. Stirner has taken the sceptre of Truth and beaten it into a pruning-hook, and now Truth, no longer an idle queen, may handle the scrubbing brush and make herself generally useful.

That Proudhon used the word egoism in a way not to make it admired makes no essential difference. There are other egoists than those who take the name.

There is some rhapsody in Proudhon, and Anarchists may note also that he puts devotion to one's country along with justice. Stirner, on the contrary, will abolish all frontiers and recognize only individuals.

I draw attention to the last of Mr. Kelly's extracts, — that Justice is not a simple notion, but that " it is also the product of a faculty or function which comes into play as soon as man finds himself in the presence of man." This is very suggestive. The men, then, are the objective realities from whose presence together justice comes as a product of a function. Is not this creating justice? Simply put, this is justice,— the result of absolute individual sovereignty, or Egoism, as I and Stirner use the term.

I will now present a few further extracts from Proudhon, taken without any long search. They are to show, firstly, that as a vivacious writer his imaginative expressions are not to be seriously weighed against his logic; and, secondly, that he does express in somewhat different terms the doctrine which I call Egoism.

I swear before God and before men, upon the Gospel and the constitution. — Probleme Sociale, p. 259.

He who by poverty has been led to steal and is punished remains forever the enemy of God and man. — Contradictions, I, p. 313.

God is stupidity and cowardice, hypocrisy and lies, tyranny and wretchedness; God is evil. — Ibid., p. 3t,0.

Charity! I deny charity; it is mysticism. Vainly you speak to me of fraternity and love. If you love me, it is through interest. Devotion! I deny devotion; it is mysticism. Speak to me of debit and credit. If I am drawn to aid you, I will do so gracefully, but I will not be obliged to. —Ibid., p. 228.

Humanism is most thorough theism. — Ibid., p. 309.

The New Philosophy, subverting method, breaking the authority of God as well as that of man, and accepting no other yoke than that of fact and evidence, makes everything converge toward the theological hypothesis as toward the last of its problems. Humanitarian atheism is, therefore, the last term of the moral and intellectual enfranchisement of man;

consequently, the last phase of philosophy, serving as a passage to the reconstruction or verification of all the demolished dogmas. — Ibid., p. 22.

Philosophy is merely a deceptive method consisting in going from the general to the particular. — De l'Ordre, p. 58.

I am in need of the hypothesis of God to justify my style. — Contradictions, I, p. 25.

A headless society, so to speak, cannot live. — Creation de l'Ordre, p. 485.

[The preceding statement was attacked by Stirner.]

But let us not blaspheme royalty, for to do so would be blaspheming humanity.—Ibid., p. 311.

Wherever religion appears, it is by no means as an organizing principle, but as a means of subjugating men's wills. — De l'Ordre, p. 17.

Respect for contracts, fidelity to one's word, the obligation of oaths, are the fictions — the ossicles, as the famed Lysander well said — with which society deceives the strong and puts them under the yoke. — Contradictions, I, p. 263.

Instead of regarding the man and his fellow, the prince and the citizen, as two terms the relation of which existed independently of consciousness and constituted the real moral law, they have imagined that this law preexisted. — De l'Ordre, p. 69.

Morality is not a science: it is an encyclopaedia. . . For, as two forces, being united, produce a complex effect quite different from the simple effect to which each one of them could give rise, and incommensurable with this, as from the combination of two simple bodies there results a composite the properties of which were not found in either of the originals. . . .

Now, just as the decisions of reason in man received the name of idea, just so the decisions of his Liberty received the name of volition, sentiments, habits, morals. Then language, figurative in its nature, continuing to supply the elements of the primary psychology, people have contracted a habit of assigning to ideas, as a place or capacity where they dwell, the intelligence; and to volitions, sentiments, etc., the consciousness. AH these abstractions have for a long time been taken by the philosophers for realities, their psychology being merely a will o' the wisp. — Contradictions.

To be a member of a democracy it is necessary in law, independently of the quality of frankness, to have made choice of the liberal system. ... As a variety of the liberal regime, I have distinguished Anarchy, or government of each one for himself. ... It consists in the fact that, political functions being reduced to industrial functions, social order would result from the sole fact of business and exchanges. Then every one would be able to term himself the autocrat of himself, which is the furthest opposite of monarchical absolutism. — Du Principe Federatif, p. l(i.

To found the society it is necessary to set forth, not simply an idea, but a judicial act. —Ibid., p. 53.

There are three modes of conceiving law, according to the point of view. ... as a believer, as a philosopher, and as a citizen. 1, Command; 2, Expression of the relation of things; 3, The arbitral statute of the human will; theory of contract. The social system to which they give rise is not the same. By the first, man declares himself subject of the law and its author or representative; by the second, he acknowledges himself an integral part of a vast organism; by the third, he makes the law his own and frees himself from all authority, fatality, and rulership. The first formula is that of the religious man; the second that of the pantheist; the third that of the republican [Anarchist]. This one alone is compatible with Liberty.—Ibid, p. 53.

The social contract extends only to exchanges. — Idee Generale, p. 118.

They have agreed among themselves mutually to keep faith and right; that is to say, to respect the rules of business which the nature of things indicates to them as alone capable of insuring them in the largest measure of welfare, safety, and peace. Will you adhere to their compact? become a part of their society? If you refuse, you are a part of the society of savages. Nothing protects you. ... If you swear to the compact, you become a part of the society of free men. —Ibid., p. 312.

Here I close, trusting that economists will especially note the extract beginning " Morality is not a science."

TAK KAK.

Noms de Plume.

Liberty, vol. 5 no. 1 (August 27, 1887): 5.

To the Editor of *Liberty*:

Miss Kelly's letter in No. 105, avowing antipathy to noms de plume, puts me in mind that there are others beside myself writing in this way. The esprit de corps, a congenial disposition, arrays me with them. Having deliberately chosen to use a nom de plume, I do not perceive the necessity for practically abandoning it at the suggestion of an opponent of noms de plume; this both for my own more immediate reasons and in solidarity with others in like case: a solidarity which I count among my instincts or characteristics. My articles are argumentative. The signature can make no difference.

Tak Kak.

Edgeworth's Miserable Insinuations.

Liberty, vol. 5 no. 4 (September 24, 1887): 5.

To the Editor of *Liberty*:

The sovereign impertinence of Edgeworth is exhibited in personal hints contained in some articles from him in the Winsted "Press," on "Anarchy vs. Egoism." Speaking of the Jay Goulds and Napoleons, Edgeworth says: "If — which I do not know to be a fact — Tak Kak is identified with these in interest and ambition, why does he let the cat out of the bag?" Now, if any one lets those villains' cat out of the bag, does it not argue that he is, if intelligent, not identified with them in interest and ambition? But Edgeworth plays with the strings of other bags and chances the letting out of other cats.

I warn Edgeworth that, if he knew me personally, he would be ashamed as long as he lives for having written some things about me. So would another of your correspondents be.

According to Edgeworth, "the humor of the thing consists in this conscienceless doctrine of successful egotism being preached to the poor devils who are perishing under its infliction by the dominant powers." Really! and is not universal individual sovereignty the cure for absolutism and usurpation?

TAK KAK.

Anarchy, Government, and Liberty.

Liberty, vol. 5 no. 6 (October 22, 1887): 6.

[J. L. W. IN THE TRUTH SEEKER.]

As an Anarchist partisan who does not think himself mentally broad enough to have surrounded all truth, I highly appreciate the work which the "Truth Seeker " is doing. From your intimation that social chaos is what you understand by Anarchy, and from reading many of your articles, I think that there is some difference in the force of certain words to your mind and ours. To me Anarchy is Liberty, and Liberty is Anarchy. You say that your party is Liberty, — Liberty for every one to think, express his thought, and act as he pleases so long as he infringes upon no other's equal right, and curtails no other's equal Liberty. Now, this is what I want, too, and with this admitted and intelligently applied we should have that condition which we call Anarchy. But I must ask that by "equal Liberty" we are at all events to understand Liberty, not equal restriction. In a tantalizing sense, there may be "equal Liberty" where there is very little Liberty. People do not yet seem to realize that, when they have put themselves under constitutional law, taking away natural Liberty, the imposition upon a dissenting minority is not redeemed by the same being submitted to by the makers. They call that equal Liberty. We call it equal slavery.

Whether or not we are to condemn government depends upon what is meant by government. Find me a government in which all the citizens have agreed to join together, and where they have the conceded right to individually withdraw from contributing to its support when it ceases to fulfil their aims, as we now have with churches, and I will admit that such government is compatible with Anarchism. Anarchists have no objection to any number of persons having a government, if such government will curtail none of our Liberty according to your definition. We say that, when a government levies taxes upon us without our consent, it curtails our Liberty and pursuit of happiness by robbing us of our means. As the churches are supported by voluntary contributions, so let the government be supported. That is to say, we have no objection to the subjects of a government voluntarily assuming such obligations and binding themselves as they see fit to contribute and to pay, but let them take nothing from us and interfere in no way with such of our acts as don't infringe upon their natural liberties, and we are content. We believe in preventing and publishing murder and robbery, etc. It is a question of words whether this prevention and punishment shall be called government or not. We refer it, when done by a hired force, to the principle of insurance.

You know that in economic science "rent" has a technical meaning. We give a technical meaning to "government." We do not use it to mean protection, but rulership. Are we not justified logically by the fact that advocates of government are constantly ready to assert that it is impossible for them to carry on their scheme without forcing all natives of the country to be citizens and taxpayers, whether they individually wish to be Bo or not ? They will respect our "equal" Liberty, but they cannot afford to respect our Liberty, neither our property. We are now in the same stage that you would be in if the idea prevailed that, in order to support the church, the majority might force the minority to be members, — at least, to contribute to it, — and that, their rights of membership, voting, etc., being reserved for them whenever they chose to claim them, they were treat-ed with " equal" religious freedom, but contribute they must and obey they must in no matter what unnecessary things the authority of the majority ordered. We are seeking to enlighten men as to the wrong and absurdity of promiscuous reciprocal tyranny. In proportion as this enlightenment spreads, the way will be prepared for that which, with your habits of thought, you may prefer to call a philosophic Anarchical government, or government of actual consent, but which we call simply An-archy. Chaos is a theological fiction. In all nature form and order result from the powers in things. Government other than self-government is violence. To have a self-governing state it would be necessary to have the voluntary adhesion of every citizen. We claim that the adhesion and support of a great ma-jority can be had for equitable regulations compatible with and in furtherance of Liberty, and that, if any stand out and cannot appreciate the benefits of insurance, we can afford to let them alone so long as they behave themselves. I claim that Anarchy will accomplish in a more true and scientific manner the aim of protection, which is all that attaches republicans to government. I claim this with the same confidence as you claim that natural morality will develop all the virtues, — for which alone some conservative people still cling to their Bibles, — and develop them far better for not having a mixture or leaven of authority foreign to the meritorious element in the case.

A Reason for Hanging Anarchists.

Liberty, vol. 5 no. 11 (December 31, 1887): 4.

The New York "World" tells its readers that Anarchy means "without a leader." The "World" has been looking in dictionaries, I infer. It finds "leader" as well as "tyrant." But nevertheless the "World" is a misleader. If the "World" had wished to explain the meaning of Anarchy as a doctrine or as an actual movement, it could have found definitions by Anarchists, and it could have noted the practices of Anarchists in association. Can it point to any exponent of Anarchy who defines it as a movement without a leader? Can the "World" give an instance from the practice of Anarchists wherein they do not avail themselves of leadership like other people? If the "World" can do neither of these things, it is convicted of ignoring what Anarchy is, and of imposing upon its readers. This course would excite scarcely any remark, if it were not for the fact that the subject is treated in no mere speculative manner in the "World," but very seriously and practically. That paper preaches against Anarchy as a crime, to be suppressed by imprisonment and hanging. The crime of being "without a leader." The mugwumps must be careful. The "World" will perhaps want them imprisoned and hanged next year.

Tak Kak.

Self-Wisdom and Egoism.

Liberty, vol. 5 no. 11 (December 31, 1887): 6.

To the Editor of *Liberty*:

"Self-wisdom" is not synonymous, not co-extensive, to my mind with intelligent Egoism. From this statement G. B. Prescott, Jr. can revise his argument. The author of the term "self-wisdom" gave no definition. Among the meanings which he may have had is this: Wisdom directed to the care of self. In this case the person has himself in view as an object. He is planning and deliberating what will build up, guard, and preserve himself,– add to his pleasures or release him from his pains. This must certainly be a large share of intelligent activity; but this is not the specific characterization of Egoism, as I use the term. Egoistic is whoever and whatever acts out the self. In writing this I am doubtless gratifying myself, but to inform Mr. Prescott is my object. Were I contemplating and working for some well-assured benefit to myself, held in prospect before my mental vision, and calculated to be the result of this writing, that would be "self-wisdom." But if I am subject, the doer, and in nowise an object to myself, the spontaneous act is Egoistic simply,– 'tis my own,–but not a matter of "self-wisdom." In such case I do not have self present to mind as an object. Now all generosity is of this character. If calculated to benefit self, it would not be generosity. The man who would never do a generous act till he had calculated it to be profitable would perhaps seem generous, but the appearance would be deceptive. The intelligent generous man must indeed learn by experience that he needs to guard against ruining himself by generosity, but, even as he grows cautious, he never needs to know more than that it is not unsafe to follow his natural bent of generosity. That is to say, he does not need the contemplation of any increment of pleasure to himself. His pleasure is: his pain as seeing suffering is: and he acts unless checked by considerations of wisdom and unwisdom, not necessarily of "self"-wisdom. If his thought is this,–to guard against against evil to others,–it is wisdom to stop and reflect whether, in a given case, it is well to follow the impulse of generosity. Now, to act so unless checked by reflection is quite different from needing the stimulus of a consciously-entertained prospect of benefit to self.

T<small>AK</small> K<small>AK</small>.

Egoism and Selfishness.

Liberty, vol. 5 no. 16 (March 10, 1888): 5.

To the Editor of *Liberty*:

Referring to the letter by G. B. Prescott, Jr., in No. 117, I would say that, if he declares that he has no purpose in writing except his own gratification, I shall not contest his statement. The distinction which he regards as irrational is to me as necessary as the words process and aim. If Mr. Prescott fully concentrates his thought upon any work, he is acting out self and gratifying self without thinking of self. This is one phase of Egoism. Mr. Prescott's sentence beginning, "To say that a man need only know — " is confused, and does not recite correctly. The next sentence beginning, "To reflect before acting—" states a negative truism never controverted by me or anyone that I know of. If Mr. Prescott cannot do better than to infer and state by implication that I had held forth that "to reflect before acting" implies studied benefit to self and harm to others, I am sorry for Mr. Prescott's understanding. Certainly retaliation is as sudden as generosity, or as often sudden. Who said that generosity was the only sudden impulse? Who said that generosity was only sudden, and not also persistent and studied? I defined my term Egoism; Mr. Prescott might define his term "selfish." Egoism, as I use the word, includes generous and ungenerous desires and conduct. It will be admitted that ungenerous is different from generous. The word "selfish" is one which is commonly used as a synonym for "ungenerous." When, therefore, a writer says that "generous impulses are selfish desires," it might be well for him to explain whether or not he means that "generous impulses" are instinctive error, and for him to define what he means by "selfish." That termination ish(?) may imply disparagement. It is worse than useless to substitute selfishness for Egoism, unless "selfishness" is defined by those who use it. As Mr. Tucker said in answer to Mr. Blodgett, "criticism of the Anarchistic idea which does not consider Anarchistic definitions is futile." It is thus that criticisms upon Egoism have been futile. Egoism is not merely an idea. It is a fact,–the force of a man untrammeled by superstition. It may be more of less generous or ungenerous; thus he may be called selfish or unselfish in the common speech. He may be more or less impulsive, more or less deliberate and reflecting. He may so feel and act as to be called very dutiful, but the Egoist relation to all objects is conditioned quite differently from that of the mentally unfree man. If he cares for others, it is not because he is taught that it is his "duty," — a teaching which puts a fetter in place of attraction; but it is because he is built that way, and this he knows.

TAK KAK.

A Difference of Words Only.

Liberty, vol. 5 no. 17 (March 31, 1888): 7.

To the Editor of *Liberty*:

I think there is no controversy between Mr. J. Wm. Lloyd and myself, though he regards "all acts as Egoistic," while I use the term Egoism, like Stirner, for acts of normal self-possession and self-expression, excluding blind crazes, fanaticism, the influence of fixed ideas, hypnotism dominating the subject and rendering him more of an automaton than of an individual, although he goes through the motions. Rewards and punishments promised and threatened appeal to the Egoism of ignorant believers, but there is also an anti-individualistic craze or fascination in religion, and love, and business, when the idea rides the man. In the last analysis it is a question of sanity or insanity. Egoism is sanity. So we use the term, and as Stirner's book, *Der Einzige und sein Eigenthum*, has long been before the world, his admirers have a good possessory title to this term.

Mr. Lloyd started to sketch the man who "needs to know," but he gives us the portrait of one who has become so far differentiated from the class that now he *knows his need*, and is actually exercising care in transforming himself, with the -conscious wish and distinct purpose to reach that condition-wherein he will no longer "need to know" at every turn that particular acts are going to be calculably profitable to him. If I admire this man for what he is making of himself, I still imply that I did not admire him for what he was.

A. — I don't like soldiers.

B. — Do not say that. Here is a worthy man. He is a soldier, but he abhors war. He has sworn never to fight except for Liberty, and to live as a civilian as soon as he can. Now, do you not like this soldier a little?

A. — I do.

Tak Kak.

A Normal Function.

Liberty, vol. 5, no. 26 (August 4, 1888): 5.

To the Editor of *Liberty*:

During the discussion on parentage it occurred to me that many men will certainly desire to contribute to the support of their children without claiming to influence the mother otherwise than by advice. Such desire is normal and healthy; and it is reasonable, kind, and honorable for the mother to allow it proper satisfaction.

TAK KAK.

Even So, What Then?

Liberty, vol. 7 no. 2 (May 24, 1890): 3.

Dear Mr. Tucker:

I have seen a statement in print that Moses Harman was arrested again for printing a letter from a doctor of medicine. If this be the arrest alluded to by you in No. 157, I regret that you did not see the number of "Lucifer" containing the provocation. I read it, and must say that it was simply a plain statement of professional experience touching on the frequency of unnatural practices indulged in by some married men, causing disease in their wives. The letter did not contain any unnecessary words for a plain statement, by a doctor, of facts in his line of business experience, the point being that a necessity exists for public attention to matters which are not so very exceptional as some people suppose. If pronounced objectionable, it can be on no other ground than the opinion that certain facts must not be made known (some will say lest information lead to imitation). If the principle of suppression be established in such a case, as the law, it will be made clear that the policy of the law is distinctly to suppress the report of vice as a fact, however coldly stated. But then what will become of the court reports?

TAK KAK.

Tak Kak Not with the "Brave."

Liberty, vol. 7 no. 4 (June 21, 1890): 7.

The brevity of my last communication might bespeak the presumption that I do not oppose your prudent policy. What! I should differ with you on a serious matter and not shed ink in argument? Impossible.

The fact that I did not enclose Dr. O'N.'s letter would go to show that I had not kept it. In attempting to describe its contents from memory, I thought only of so much as bore upon liability to prosecution and arousing the spirit which resorts to persecution. When I perused the letter, my attention was upon that question or feature, and my recollection, according to the natural law of memory, was conned to what I had taken interest in noting. In saying if pronounced objectionable," I meant by repressionists.

Mr. Harman had published effusions from non-professional people. A doctor's letter signed with his name and more nearly on the line of fact might seem to have a better chance of being privileged. Now while, for the purpose of illustration, the mention of a certain book simplifies your argument, in which I agree, yet I would not leave the slightest possibility for any reader to misclass Mr. Harman. To publish anything in pure deance is a radical error in policy. To publish a thing with a sincere trust in the reason of the people who sustain prosecutions, appealing all the while to their reason and believing, however mistakenly, that they cannot resist the evidence of truth and utility, is an error of judgment when its result is nally no better than this in the Harman case thus far. There may, however, be thousands of comparatively fair-minded men who will aid in getting Mr. Harman his Liberty if they are made to know that his error has been of the last mentioned of these classes, not of the rest.

Tak Kak.

[I am glad that the discussion of this subject has revealed a substantial agreement between Tak Kak and myself. And I certainly am as far as he from any desire to misclass Mr. Harman. The parenthetical remark in my original paragraph was especially intended as a precaution against that.—Editor *Liberty*.]

The Question of Copyright.—I.

Liberty, vol. 7 no. 22 (February 21, 1891): 5.

I have read with interest what has appeared in *Liberty* on this subject,—no doubt a puzzling one, because both abstract and complex. What is copyright? The word means the light to copy. But if I say I am in favor of copying what we want to copy, the advocates of copyright will immediately tell me that this is precisely what they do not allow, except to the author or his assigns. The word and the law are derived from a political condition in which the sovereign prohibited individual activities in general, then relaxed the prohibition in favor of certain persons. This theory of despotic power and gracious indulgence is the foundation of the patent system. The author is one of the class of inventors, otherwise discoverers. Whether he had to labor to any appreciable extent or whether his discovery, his prose or poetry, ashed from his genius, makes no dierence in his standing as regards his legal right.

Starting from the Egoistic point of view, I of course have no respect for his right as his right. Is it convenient to me in the long run? By a process of reasoning and some inherited qualities I perceive, and it is agreeable to me to feel, that men may be approximately equal in industrial relations with mutual benet. Thus I am disposed to allow to others the possession of their labor products if they will allow mine to me. But I make no sacred dogma of this, and it has to be qualied in accordance with my reason for allowing it. Thus, for example, if my neighbor takes a notion to make a garden upon the ground devoted to a road, I shall consult my own convenience about driving across his garden.

I not only allow to others their labor products, but also a reasonable amount of material on which to work, and all material in which they have embodied their labor without trespass. Both these kinds of property I cheerfully recognize, as being inseparable. Here I am disposed to stop. Show me that any other property is reasonable and can be maintained without government; then I may acknowledge it.

Literary and patent-right property, as I know it, is another name for prohibition. It prohibits an exercise of one's imitative and laboring faculties. It is true that I will join with my neighbor B to prevent C from taking B's farm or his status or his house, and I expect general consent. Why? Because men in general can make use of land for farms, and can enjoy property in the other mentioned forms. It is not especially because he chiseled the statue or built the house, but because it came into his possession in a manner which I recognize as lawful, perhaps by ex- change. There appears to be enough raw material for all to have work and consequent comfort. All men can find use for a piece of land: hence, when men become more intelligent, they will see their interest in defending the occupier. But how many out of a thousand are capable of availing themselves of copyright and patent laws to make more than they can make by disregarding such laws?

All men have labor products limited by the material in which the labor is embodied, and hence transferable. A copyright privilege or patent-right privilege awaits embodiment in other material, and the author or inventor, if protected, can but levy toll upon those who will embody it in imitation of him.

I see that it is proposed, in putting together the scattered provisions of the British copyright law, to include abridgments. Then there is the right of translation. Plagiarism is a delicate point in many cases. I think it must be very difficult to contrive any plan of protecting copyright which will not either leave a loophole for plagiarism or involve government, and that such would be the case were all disposed to admit the doctrine of copyright.

As a matter of comity, I think publishers could well come to agreements not to duplicate each other's work, but an indispensable condition among free men must be that authors and their publishers shall not enjoy the prohibitory privilege which is the soul of copyright.

Besides indorsing Mr. Tucker's argument in reply to Mr. Donisthorpe, I wish to add a few words on the inventions which have been abandoned to the public, not superseded. Let us suppose that perpetual patent and copyright had existed from the beginning of civilization, and that all inventors had claimed their "rights." In that case there would be royalties on the wheel, the saw, the knife, the axe, the plough, the use of iron, the processes in every manufacture, on all games, on money, on paper, on re, on matches, on window glass, on doors and hinges, on springs, on locks, on beds, on soap and the use of soap, on hot water, on brushes, on every kind of clothes and shoes, on ink, types and every press, on the musical notation, on books, on the alphabet, on the numerals, on arithmetic, on bookkeeping by single and double entry. What would business men do without gures? They must pay the descendant of some Arabian. What would engineers do without algebra? They, too, must pay. Everybody must pay for having a name and surname. What would composers do without a staff and notes, or authors without an alphabet? They could not claim any copyright, for they are using signs invented by a monk. The Church, being his heir, might farm letters out. But it, in turn, must get the permission of the owners of the processes of paper-making, printing, and bookbinding. The whole system, besides, would require more functionaries than Proudhon enumerated to bedevil the mass of mankind. Can that be social science which would result in slavery to privilege but for the abandonments and invasions before social science was thought of?

Mr. Simpson's proposition of control over another by virtue of having adorned his piece of land, and the other's wanting to imitate his adornment, will do very well. I shall imitate Mr. Simpson's adornment and make no pretence of originality or coincidence. In order to ne me, he will have to come with force upon my piece of land. I shall talk to the neighbors about it, and endeavor to show them how the balance of exchange is affected if we do not receive labor equivalents, but are forced to pay for looking at objects publicly exposed. Mr. Simpson will then proceed to enforce his claim, perhaps. While he is doing so, I may have the luck to discover in the property of somebody else the natural object which gave him his de- sign, and then there will be an unlimited claim against Mr. Simpson.

I have some further remarks to make touching on Spencer and Yarros.

Tak Kak.

Hare and Tortoise.

Liberty, vol. 7 no. 22 (February 21, 1891): 7.

Mr. Simpson has allowed himself to be caught by a sophist's trick, since he believes that logicians have failed to disprove the logical impossibility of a bare overtaking a tortoise if the tortoise gets a slight start. Given the number of yards constituting the start, the speed of the bare, and the speed of the tortoise, there can be no trouble in demonstrating how soon the hare will overtake the tortoise; but, if I might impose the condition under which the demonstration shall be made, I could contrive so that Mr. Simpson should never be able to reach the conclusion. The sophist's trick referred to is to contemplate the bare going half the distance given as a start, while the tortoise goes a shorter distance; then half the remainder; then half that still remains, and so on, thus consuming time and refusing to deal with the whole problem. To prevent the demonstration of any proposition, it would only be necessary to require that the demonstrator shall consume a minute in writing the first word, two minutes in writing the second word, and so on. until years would elapse, and he would die before he could get to the conclusion.

TAK KAK.

Sentimental and Incomplete.

Liberty, vol. 7 no. 23 (March 7, 1891): 1.

[Tak Kak in Egoism.]

Reading the article by Mr. Westrup on "Scientific, Against Religious Methods" I agree with him that Mr. Pentecost's treatment of the interest question is unsatisfactory. It is not only because a sentimental consideration predominates in Mr. Pentecost's presentation of the case, but also because that presentation is very incomplete.

The man who by economy and self-denial has saved $1,000 has probably done much more than $1,000 worth of work in exchange for that sum. His labor products are somewhere in the mass of wealth and not his possession. While he has the money there exists a suspense account between him and capitalistic society. Let us assume that it has 81,500 of his product. If now necessity compels him to spend his $1,000 for immediate support, he has lost $500 worth of his labor. But say this man is not compelled to spend his $1,000. So much the better for him. He has been underpaid in amount, but paid in a privileged money. The possession of it affords him a prospect or chance of ultimately getting $1,500 worth of products, — or what he has earned. We can leave out of account the unscientific nature of the arrangement, which may give him more or less, while we are analyzing a pretence that the man is not entitled to more than $1,000 worth of products. The persons who paid him in money could not pay him in full, because money was with them a scarce thing. They paid him a sum with a potentiality of recovering from society the balance due him if he can wait. This is one point which Mr. Pentecost has not considered.

If now he lends his money at interest he is told that he will be appropriating from among the borrower's goods a sum that he will have done nothing to earn. Has the borrower no judgment about that? The lender who saved "by economy and self-denial" has already earned more than he lends if he lends without interest, for he has earned $1,000 worth of scarce, interest-commanding money, which is a very different thing from earning $51,000 in a free currency that would represent only labor value and that value fully paid up at the time. But the principal thing to which I now wish to direct further attention is in this question: from whose goods is the interest taken? Mr. Pentecost says from the borrower, and he means it strictly, of course, for he suggests a loan without interest; a loan, mark, of this very monopoly money which one has worked disadvantageously to get. But the fact that the borrower pays the interest and has more left than he would have if the loan had been refused, may be deemed proof that the interest does not come out of the borrower's goods. It comes out of the general stock of wealth through the borrower. One must smile when one hears the assertion that the borrower under the present regimen performs for the lender a service for no equivalent. The borrower who could get money without interest would compete with others who have to pay interest and would put so much more profit in his pocket.

To view this subject the better let us suppose that the owner of the $1,000 locks it up instead of lending it. Mr. Pentecost has aroused the man's conscientious scruples or his pride and he will not take interest, but he does not feel in duty bound to lend, neither willing to allow another to perform a gratuitous service for him, and after all he is not such a ninny as to pay the borrower for taking his precious mono- poly money and exploiting society with it. So he does no- thing. Now society has provided little currency and has not calculated upon men's refusing interest, what will be the effect of locking the money up? That the would-be borrower may seek elsewhere, with a tendency to higher interest; that some labor seeking employment will come to a stand; and that while the owner of the money will not draw from the general store any products in excess of $1,000 valuation, the interruption of labor caused by his withdrawal from circulation of $1,000 in money under present circumstances will arrest production so as to leave the total stock smaller than it would have been if he had accepted interest and let the money go into circulation. These points also Mr. Pentecost does not touch upon, yet they concern one taking any comprehensive view on the subject.

There is one expression used by Mr. Westrup which is perhaps questionable. He says: "It is the very essence of Egoism that if the ends sought by Altruists are ever attained they will be reached through Egoism." I think that nothing which is contingent or doubtful can be logically of the es- sence of Egoism. But I will take it that Mr. Westrup means: the essence of Egoism is such that an inference may be drawn to the effect mentioned. With this understanding Egoism is logically as independent of any process of negation or deliverance from altruistic dogmas as Freethought is in- dependent of any negation or deliverance from the dogmas of Christian or other theology. The transition stage, however, presents certain phenomena in modes of expression and in eagerness by the individual to vindicate his new tenets with special comparisons. A general unconcern about any sort of Altruism that does not seem to interfere with the enjoyment of life will be found to characterize the mature Egoistic mind. With Mr. Pentecost Egoism is probably as yet a theory rather than a condition — a theory which be perhaps understands well enough and which he would have applied better if he had looked carefully into the complicated question of money as it is.

Copyright.—II.

Liberty, vol. 7 no. 23 (March 7, 1891): 5–6.

Mr. Yarros is an easy writer. A proverb tells the consequence to readers. He began on copyright by designating the "notion " of a perpetual monopoly of ideas as "too silly to require any force for its refutation." But in his second article he says that "it is only the difficulties in the practical application of the general principle that necessitate the abridgment and limitation of the right of property in this particular sphere," and, as to the perpetual and unlimited right to property in ideas, "there is no argument against such a monopoly which does not apply equally well to monopoly in things material produced by labor." In his third article, he claims by the general principle of equal Liberty property in ideas as having "the same sanction as property in material things," and says: " In no case does the author or inventor who has the monopoly of the use or sale of his invention or discovery infringe the equal right of others." But the application of the principle is difficult, hence "where absolute justice cannot be had" a temporary protection is accorded. As to literary works he says: "I see no reason for violating the general principle in this case." Now then, was it excessively silly (if all this be so) for anyone to entertain the notion of a perpetual monopoly of ideas, at least until the practical breakdown of the general principle was discovered? Is it too silly a notion to need refutation, though Mr. Yarros's refutation does not directly affect the notion, but affects a line of conduct? Can every one be expected to know off-hand when a general principle must be *violated?*

I gather that Mr. Yarros believes in two kinds of copyright : perpetual as to the exact form, and temporary as to the ideas,— temporary protection against plagiarism. In saying "ideas," I am reminded of a question how far form of expression is idea and how far it is labor. I feel quite certain that it is both combined in varying proportions; but, to proceed, I will say of form, to eliminate all question of coincidence, here is a book with the author's name on the title page.

Mr. Yarros professes to diverge from the Spencerian position,—to make a distinction between the right to property in inventions and the right to literary property. Was it not an unnecessary distinction to be paraded in front of Mr. Tucker in view of the fact that Mr. Tucker was not attacking merely perpetual copyright and patent right but the temporary right also,—and in view of the fact that Mr. Yarros believes in the right of protection in the one case for some time and in the other for all time? Tucker is after the Canaanites and the Amalekites, whereupon Yarros comes in and says: I perceive a distinction. These are not all Amalekites!

The alleged divergence of Mr. Yarros from Spencer appears to consist not in a distinction between copyright, in the broad sense in which Spencer uses the word, and patent right, but in a distinction which leaves a great deal of copyright still in the same category with patent right and separates one conceivable kind or degree of copyright from the rest so remaining with patent right. Though Spencer does not make that distinction, there is nothing to show that he would be unwilling to make it. Had Mr. Yarros repudiated property in ideas and held to property in the form, there would have been a difference between him and Spencer instead of there being simply a distinction in that he analyzes a point which Spencer leaves untouched, but which Spencer's argument would lead Spencer to analyze to the same effect were be considering copyright more minutely and not with relation to first the general principle and secondly his expedient abandonment of the general principle on account of practical difficulty. But were Spencer making such distinction, he would not call this a distinction between patent right and copyright, but a distinction between (1) that copyright which protects against plagiarism and with this all patent rights, and (2) that copyright which might be given to an author for his work say with his name on the title page.

Says Mr. Yarros: "I cannot follow Spencer in his attempt to abridge the right of authors to their literary works." Yet Mr. Yarros has avowed himself in favor of abridging something which goes by the name of copyright — the protection of a monopoly in ideas — which is what Spencer had in view, as witness the quotation from Spencer made by Mr. Yarros. Spencer speaks of "new knowledge," being claimed as private property, of "property in ideas," which "it seems difficult to specify," and thereupon he couples the inventor and author together, "patent and copyright." All this shows that the abridgment spoken of was conceived with reference to that element in copyright which protects property in ideas.

On the Spencerian argument itself, I will claim a hearing in another article, but I will now draw attention to these facts, namely, that whereas Spencer introduces assertions with the phrases: "It is tolerably self-evident," "It is clear," "It is further manifest," Mr. Yarros predicates that "property in ideas is logically deduced by Spencer from the principle of equal Liberty." Spencer's language does not lead me to think that Spencer would make quite this claim. He finds himself prepossessed in favor of property in ideas, and, as far as shown by the quotations, he does not perceive any violation of Liberty in reaping a harvest from the activity of others whom he may assume to have been aided by the ideas. He does not see the harm of the method by which the man who supplies the idea is aided to secure his alleged share in the results of its application. The most I make of Spencer's position as viewed by Spencer is that he thinks property in ideas is not vetoed by the principle of equal Liberty; and included in his notion of property in ideas is a projection of power which I shall not admit to be part of the science of industrial relations.

Tak Kak.

Copyright.—III.

Liberty, vol. 7 no. 24 (March 21, 1891): 4–5.

In *Liberty* No. 176 there are two quotations from Herbert Spencer, the first claiming new knowledge as private property, and the second discussing the probability of independent discoveries as a reason for limiting the inventor's monopoly. I regard Mr. Tucker's reply in the same number as being satisfactory, but there is perhaps occasion for a review of the alleged property in ideas and of copyright in every form, from the point of view of individual possession as true property versus societary invasion of the individual to establish an alleged property.

My thoughts are my property as the air in my lungs is my property. When I publish my ideas, they become the property of as many persons as comprehend them. If any person wishes to live by imparting his ideas in exchange for labor, I have nothing to say against his doing so and getting cooperative protection without invading the persons and property of myself and my allies. We will take care, if we can, that he and his party do not invade our houses, stop our printing-presses, and seize our books. Mr. Spencer is welcome to all the property in ideas that he can erect and maintain without government. No one can speak or write, and yet have the same advantage as if he were silent, plus the advantage of a market for his lecture or his book, even if he sell but one copy. But whatever he can do by contract, cooperation, and boycotting,—that is, by the means of equal Liberty,—let him do at his pleasure.

When Spencer claims the "exclusive use" of his original ideas, I am interested to know how he purposes of enforcing such claim. I do not admit it. The mere fact that the idea was original with him does not have an effect to debar me from using it after he communicates it to me. I do not invade any privacy, but, when he either sells or gives me knowledge, it is mine. It is simply impossible for him to have property in me, — in the restraint of me so that I must not use my pen, my paper, and Mr. Tucker's type with Mr. Tucker's consent; — that is to say, all this is impossible without tyranny. The terms equal freedom, if construed to mean an equal degree of freedom and an equal degree of denial of freedom,— that is, less than full freedom, — become a mockery of what I understand by equal freedom. I understand by it no privileged order of persons, no privilege except by personal consent. And here is the point: if I undertake to limit my conceivable action, I do so in the exercise of my freedom to choose or refuse alliance with others. Further, while choosing as wise and congenial to outlaw the robber, the thief, and the murderer, in asking only voluntary adhesion to the Anarchistic compact we recognize that adhesion is an exercise of freedom. I would be understood that property, in the alleged invasion of which I may be taken, is to be given no idealistic extension. Otherwise I will not sign the compact, for the terms equal *Liberty* will mean no more than reciprocal invasion.

This result follows: there are two associations where there would have been one. Owing to Mr. Yarros's association demanding for authors a prohibition upon printers, perhaps many authors adhere to it; but the printers will probably adhere to the same association as myself. I can understand that men who feel that their property is invaded will retaliate, but I do not understand how the authors are going to retaliate successfully against the printers and readers. I know that the pensioners regard their incomes as property and are prepared to keep themselves saddled upon the taxpayers, and it is possible that some pensions have been given for services which some of the taxpayers would willingly contribute something to reward, but only as a voluntary contribution. On a claim to exact the pensions, the issue depends upon the decision of those who pay them.

Anarchism has to face the claims of people who have put the evidences of past labor into government bonds and land investments as well as patent and other royalties. It is very important then to settle the question: what constitutes property?

I take a copyrighted book and copy it. I give or sell the copy to another. He reads it. He might or might not have bought the author's edition if I had never existed to draw his attention to the work. All that I do in the matter is done in my own room and with my own property.

The author does not know of my action, and cannot, by

any inspection of his property, discover that any part is missing. Does not the analysis show that the claim of immaterial literary property is a claim of property in other men's production? True that but for the author the book would not be there for me to copy, but true also that I have not contracted with any man to give him a power of thrusting his partnership upon me, he doing something which has cost him certain labor and in return taking a general injunction upon us all, from which it is not impossible that he will make ten thousand times the amount that his labor would have made. This, if we permit, he makes out of us by the combination of a certain amount of labor with some fortunate idea and our belief in allowing immaterial property. Do we not all see that here are the elements of exploitation of man by man? And under Anarchism will not the authors' association be so small and the free copyright association so large that the former will find it expedient to disband on making some terms for consideration that will give the author a reasonable return for his labor, not at all a recognized right to make all he can by the means of a social prohibition? His own individual prohibition would mostly be impotent.

To steal is to take by stealth, — without the knowledge and consent of the owner. As long as Spencer has an idea in his brain, it is his, and it is not mine until it is in my brain. I do not get it by stealth if he publishes it. I shall then print his idea in his own words; make an exact copy of his book, with his name on the title-page, if it suits me best to do so.

If the printer may not copy new books, of course the shoemaker may not copy new shoes. But that would be the denial of Liberty. The equality would be in the denial and frustration of Liberty, not in the Liberty. There is also denial of property where there is denial of Liberty. The new shoe or the new book has superseded the old ones, and the shoemaker or printer with materials and tools in hand must copy what is in demand or starve. If he be not permitted to use his tools and his material in fashioning any goods that he knows how to fashion, and chooses to fashion, his Liberty and his property are frustrated at one stroke. The old forms are no longer marketable. The choice is between these two: making him the slave of the man of new ideas or leaving him a free man. If the man of new ideas kept his new ideas to himself, the shoemaker or printer would at least have work, for the public would be content with fresh supplies of what it had before.

Ask for some agreement or arrangement which will secure a reward to the inventor or author, but do not ask for recognition of exclusive property in ideas when they have been made common, for that is falsehood, contradiction in terms. Ask for reward in any form rather than by the stale, execrable device of preventing production, — a method radically contrary to Liberty.

Liberty for the printer and the shoemaker puts them in the same boat, though there is the difference that a copying of Herbert Spencer's works or any other books, from title-page to *finis*, means a flat denial of property in restrictive privilege, whereas the shoe may he invented by another, no one knows how soon. The argument of Mr. Tucker is a "settler": that one who has seen an invention is debarred in that respect from becoming an inventor. It may be seen also that the author by writing a certain book has probably cut some one else out from writing a different book with successful results.

This leads to another consideration. If the author is entitled to property in his so-called "work,"— the immaterial "book,"— a projection and exploitation, not really *proper* to him but a power of society,— than he may be held responsible for all damage done by his "property" running at large. The Liberty of the press will be a serious thing for authors when they are held responsible for the action of their alleged property,—their oxen that gore, and steam-engines that explode, and poisons that destroy. Shall we have even more government?

In my second article I accommodated myself for the moment to Mr. Yarros's terminology as to the more general ideas (contra, plagiarism) and literary form, respectively; but I must say that both what to express and how to express it are certainly ideas. The words as material signs, ink on paper, are all thereabout that is not ideal. When we speak of labor of production in this matter of ideal form, we speak of labor which is precedent to obtaining the form. There may be much labor in obtaining some ideas which, when obtained, present no difficulty in variously expressing them, a number of facts, for instance, which may be stated in figures, words, or Roman numerals; and there may be little labor expended in the manner of expressing an idea even when it appears that long and hard labor would be requisite for another person to express it in that manner. In poetry, for example, often there is scarcely the ghost of an idea other than that of the arrangement of the words, and we know not whether the arrangement has cost a day's labor more than copying would have cost. When we speak of the manner of expressing an idea, we deceive ourselves if we forget that manner is ideal. It is convenient to speak of tools and material, but this does not alter the fact that the adze and the trowel are themselves material. Manner in the ideal is the tool with which ideas of fact are arranged or shaped. Though thus distinguished, it is to be identified ultimately in ideal basis with ideal material, as the material tool is to be identified in basis with the material material. In short, it is as illogical to contrast literary expression with ideas as to contrast grapes with fruit. But the labor? Well, the labor of arranging a bouquet of wild flowers may be more apparent: it is not more actual than the labor of discovering the flowers to be arranged.

I cannot admit that labor of production is better attested in a collocation of words than in a mechanical invention. The demonstrable labor in writing is that which the copyist would have to duplicate. The labor in making a model may be less than in writing a volume, but in neither case do we see all the forms that have been constructed or know of all the mental efforts that have been made.

We meet people who are sure they know what to say, but not how to express it. Expression is terribly hard work for them. Such people either deceive themselves, or they are trying to deceive others as to their knowledge, or they really want to appropriate from some other person the full expression of the ideas which they have partly appropriated, but to do it in some slight disguise, and to be paid for it, not as copyists, but as authors, be their aim even only social estimation.

Labor indispensably prerequisite to production is labor without which the product would not have come into being. It may be labor in gathering ideas of fact or labor of arranging ideas of relation, — literary expression for one kind. In either case it is labor of production of the first product. Without discovery, no product; often, without labor, no discovery.

What is the right to use and abuse? It is intelligible as the definition of personal material possessions and of ideas as possessed in the individual consciousness. Thus the owner of types may employ them in any way (use or abuse). But what becomes of the right to abuse if one may not abuse in every way? My idea of the "right to abuse" is not that we approve abuse, but that we recognize possession and individual immunity from interference in the handling. Liberty to do all acts consistent with the equal Liberty of others implies that each may possess materials and employ them as he sees fit, short of injuring another in his life, Liberty, or property (possessions). How can I lessen or injure him in his idea, general or particular, or say his form of expression, by repeating it? I can injure his project of exploitation by reasoning against it. Hence, if protection to "literary property" be needed, it may be necessary to disfavor my Liberty of discussion.

After literary property and the copyright protective system come personal reputation and the law of libel. I am but a limited owner of pen and paper if I may not attack reputations. I throw this out by way of suggestion for others to reflect upon. My own view of equal Liberty and property admits of no breakdown or exception in the "general principle." I hold to tangible possessions and personal immunity in what I deem use of tongue, pen, and all industrial appliances. Ownership of the press means more than the so-called Liberty of the press which is the "right to use." It means the exercise which all others may call abuse; and it is for ownership that I contend, which excludes all claims to tribute or involuntary partnership, and logically requires me to view ownership strictly as personal possession. A convenient test is this: No ownership except in that which is embodied in tangible form, hence subject to wear and decay, for this is the general mark of products as distinct from that so-called production which can be imparted to others and become common property without the original owner having less than before,— the ideal, hence simply discovery.

I must criticise an attempt to employ the word monopoly

to designate personal possession. The word monopoly is properly used to designate an exclusive privilege of market, and how could this be more glaringly exemplified than it is when one has an immaterial so-called "property," so that he sells nothing but a permit and does not reduce the quantity of what he has to sell when he makes a sale? By making use of the word monopoly as a forced synonym for that true property which is personal possession, a sort of color is given to the notion that monopoly might be equitable property.

What appears of the fabulous possibilities of wealth suggested in selling permits to successive generations will stamp ideal "production" as discovery beyond doubt, and thus as being outside the sphere of industrial production with its labor equivalents of perishable and consumable products. The imperishable and inconsumable were never produced in the sense of equitable commerce.

Mr. Yarros's hint as to introducing a different kind of copyright induces me to remark that, while this use of language is common, it is not penetrating. The differences now existing relate to time and extent of territory, hence are only by a loose use of language called different kinds, — meaning copyright variously conditioned. Now, if Mr. Yarros were to introduce voluntary associative methods in procuring consent to copyright, that would be a difference as to mode of execution rather than as to the right claimed.

TAK KAK.

A Century of Fraud.

Liberty, vol. 8 no. 11 (August 22, 1891): 3.

I have glanced at the August issue of the "Century Magazine," which gives a history of the Argentine cedule. I have also read in a cursory manner the May article. I see that the whole series is so much claptrap to catch the credulous, — a conclusion not surprising. I had seldom looked in the "Century," having long since summed it up as a publication calculated to render leisure hours pleasant for certain classes. And we know that with those classes the necessity is not to breach any disagreeable truth; while at critical times a voluntary contribution to their armory of falsehood is probably accepted as a luxury and may lead to distribution of numerous copies among the voters.

If the account given of the Rhode Island bank by McMaster and by the "Century" writer might be accepted, there was nothing in the scheme the failure of which can reflect on free banking. They say it was a chartered monopoly from the first, and that the borrowers were allowed to have quantities of paper money far exceeding the value of the security pledged, — which course would seem to show that the management did not aim to keep the paper at par with coin. One may suspect that there was treason in the bank organization to damn the principle misrepresented. If not so at first, and if the story as told in the "Century" be true, then soon after there was a conspiracy with the State. It is said that the General Assembly "came to the aid of the bank. . . . A forcing act was passed subjecting any person who should refuse to take the bills in payment for goods on the same terms as specie, or should in any way discourage their circulation in such terms, to a fine of £100 and to the loss of his rights as a freeman. This made matters worse than ever."

Naturally, but we do not know whether or not the statesmen and specie bankers of that time had the General Assembly "come to the aid" of the Land Bank quite as a second -and more powerful footpad comes to the aid of the victim who is struggling in the embrace of footpad number one, — quite as the "Century Magazine" comes "to the aid" of seekers of economic information.

TAK KAK.

Must the Ego Count Himself Out?

Liberty, vol. 8 no. 25 (November 28, 1891): 3.

[Tak Kak in Egoism.]

Self-interest masks itself and says suavely "we seek the good of the species," instead of saying bluntly "we gladly pick up all that other individuals let slip from their grasp." Are not we the species as contradistinguished from any individual? When we go so far as to urge sacrifices for the good of the species, what are we but beggars and hypocrites? Persuasion is mingled freely with flattery administered to the vanity of the individual, and it is not to be ignored that the Moral philosopher flatters himself as he proceeds to render what he vainly imagines to be a service to his species. Assuming the point of view that be is spokesman for the species is a subtle mendicancy or a veiled terror in the sup- posed interest of the crowd. But, assuming an individual point of view, the question is differently shaped. It then becomes: what use can I make of the species, of the crowd?

A summary of ethical teachings by Herbert Spencer says that postulating the desirability of the preservation and prosperity of the given species, there emerges the general conclusion that "in order of obligation the preservation of the species takes precedence of the preservation of the individual." The species, he admits, "has no existence save as an aggregate of individuals," and hence " the welfare of the species is an end to be subserved only as subserving the welfare of individuals," but, continues the summary, "since disappearance of the species involves absolute failure in achieving the end, whereas disappearance of individuals makes fulfillment simply somewhat more difficult, 'the preservation of the individual must be subordinated to the preservation of the species where the two conflict.'"

There are several features of sophistry in this. Let us, however, note first the admission that "the species" is simply a convenient term. Now, where confusion is possible the safe way is to lay aside the term. When this is done it will be found that in restating the foregoing propositions it becomes necessary to speak, instead, either of all the individuals concerned except one or of all the individuals concerned, without exception. But he has seemingly used the term species in both senses, or else, with his "order of obligation" he has affirmed an obligation to subordinate the preservation of one individual to that of another. As this is intelligible for the purpose of the crowd dealing with individuals but not for the individual acting for himself with himself as the victim, the immediate inference at this point is that Spencer is expounding the Egoistic logic of the crowd.

If the welfare of others is subserved only as subserving my welfare, it can never be true that I must subordinate my preservation to that of others, for this is to use the general rule, which applies while I am one of the crowd, to the exceptional case wherein I am set apart from the crowd. All conditions of benefit imply at least preservation. When I am counted out for non-preservation, for the good of others, it must be the others, not I, who do the counting out. In the first premise Spencer speaks for the individual treating the crowd from his proper motive; but in the conclusion he speaks for the crowd or some of its preserved part contemplating the sacrifice of an individual, yet these shifting points of view are included in a syllogism. The welfare of the crowd a mediate end: that is reasonable to the individual. The preservation of the individual a mediate end to the crowd: that is reasonable from the crowd': point of view; but analysis of the diverse points of view is needed, not an attempt to link the two in a syllogism the conclusion of which is merely the crowd's conclusion.

Now examine the second premise of the syllogism: "the disappearance of the species involves absolute failure in achieving the end." Why, in fact? Because the disappearance of all others of the species but myself involves it? Not at all; but because the term species includes myself. But as far as my existence is concerned it would be the same if I alone disappeared. Do you say: the preservation of the alphabet is of no use to A except as A combines with the letters: but the disappearance of the alphabet would involve the disappearance of A; hence the preservation of one letter (A) is less important than the preservation of all the other letters? The letter A answers: "Bosh!"

Speaking for the individual, how does the doctrine of subordination of the preservation of the individual accord with evolutionary theory regarding the origin of species? Do species originate by individuals taking care of themselves under whatever circumstances, if possible, or by the contrary rule of the benevolence toward the pro-existing species? The reader can pursue this inquiry for himself: but I should like to suggest that what has been considered regarding the individual and the species can be paraphrased with reference to the species and the genus under which it is classied, thus:

The welfare of the genus is to be subserved only as subserving the welfare of the species, but since the disappearance of the genus involves absolute failure, whereas disappearance of particular species makes fulfillment simply somewhat more difficult, therefore the preservation of the species must be subordinated to the preservation of the genus where the two conflict. The fallacy of this sort of reasoning may appear without comment, in as much as the individual will easily maintain the point of view of the interested species, and will not practically allow himself to slide over to the position of the presuming genus. A supplementary remark may be indulged. The genus never licenses or encourages the origination of new species; but then the verbal sophistry of the genus would not prove to be a preventive.

Egoism or Self-Sacrifice?

Liberty, vol. 8 no. 36 (February 13, 1892): 2–3.

The individualist torch of "Today" flickers in the gust of sentiment as one throws open the door of the idol's temple, whereas
it has mostly burned to illuminate with the steady light requisite for analysis.

In a criticism of Spencerian doctrine, on a point illustrating Egoism, I wrote: "If the welfare of others is subserved only
as subserving my welfare, it can never be true that I must subordinate my preservation to that of others;" for non-preservation would frustrate future welfare; and I expressed the view
that there is no apparent way to account consistently and clear-
ly for Spencer's simultaneously making of the species nothing
but a utility for the individual and making the preservation of
the species take precedence of that of the individual "in order
of obligation,"—without some change of point of view.

I more particularly criticised Spencer's middle link of alleged reason why (that the disappearance of the species would
include the disappearance of the individual), and I may now
add that it seems wholly inconsistent with his placing the individual in contradistinction to the species, which relation implies mutual exclusion. I may also add that much action having
some tendency to help or hurt large numbers of the species
has to be examined before we can know whether or not it will
involve harm, and what harm', to a given individual. May I
not presume that the alleged "obligation" to serve the species
will operate nevertheless when somewhat less than every living
soul of the species is involved?

"Today" accepts Spencer's utterances, but throws little light
on them. It speaks of "the principle which holds of creatures
leading solitary lives" and adds that this receives qualification
in the case of gregarious creatures. Does "Today" think that,
when Spencer wrote "the welfare of the species is to be subserved only as subserving the welfare of individuals," he was
speaking only of "creatures leading solitary lives"? As for the
"qualification" in the case of gregarious creatures, "Today" is ex-
cusable for its supposition regarding my lack of understanding,
but it shall have an opportunity of seeing preceding articles of

my series in the publication entitled "Egoism," in which has been illustrated more than a "qualification" of the original and safe principle. There is viable evidence on every hand of lapses from sound reason through the stealthy influence of ideas becoming fixed and dominant. That which is at first a means becomes an end, the sense of proportion being overthrown, and we have irrational action. Whether "society," or an alluring person, or a phantom of enormous wealth, or a mere hobby be the object, there is the like tendency to an overthrow of rational individual self-control.

"Today" says that I ignore "the facts generalized." I do not wish to ignore them. I do not ignore the fact that enthusiasts sometimes count themselves out for non-preservation. Some of them prefer to preserve a creed, or national honor, or reverence for an emperor, rather than their own life. I have assisted to generalize many such facts. The bipeds whose I conduct furnishes the facts of a virtual insanity are not representative of adherence to individuality, but while language remains what it is, "Today" can term them "Egos." I speak for myself and am permitted in this to represent other facts,—some of us think of later evolution and of surviving power,—when I declare that "when I am counted out for non-preservation, for the good of others, it must be the others, not I, who do the counting out." "Today" objects that I have assumed: " all conditions of benefit imply at least preservation," and this assumption will not do. The trouble is, I haven't Mr. Spencer's elegant knack of ringing in a phrase,—"it is manifest"; "almost self-evident"; "there emerges the general conclusion," etc.; but, as a slight compensation, perhaps, my simple compositions are comparatively free from the array of question-begging sign-posts. People can take me to task. You can not do so with a writer who is careful enough not to be quite sure of anything. Of course I was wrong if the words "all conditions of benefit" mean no more than all benefits. All benefits do not imply preservation, for I remember reading that on the battle-field one officer gave another the merciful pistol shot which ended his suffering. I thank "Today" for the suggested correction, but it will have a poor opinion, I fear, of an Egoist's gratitude as I proceed to make use of it. A valuable discovery, this! Decidedly, some conditions, not of personal benefit, — unhappy conditions, — demand non-preservation. Hence suicide; the Carthaginians throw themselves into the flames; the young brave rushes to hopeless battle under the shame of disaster. Life is too painful for voluntary continuance. If "Today" had not corrected(?) me in this minor premise, it might have claimed a great many self-sacrificing acts as being altruistic or even Altruistic, which acts now must seem doubtful of classification because we have not the facts of personal consciousness which immediately preceded them, and, for all that we know, the self-sacrificing individual was suffering a pain that drove him frantic, while spectators thought, judging merely by appearances, and not knowing the bottom facts, that he was doing a high, heroic act.

It is curious in several aspects that "Today" should seek to set aside my minor premise. The major, by Spencer, is a conclusive enunciation, and it is not apparent what connected use "Today" could make of the setting aside but to immediately enlarge its recognition of some facts of surrender as being possibly Egoic, whereas "Today" had before assumed otherwise; and finally, on this score, the logic, whatever it ought to be, may apply to the species. Suppose Spencer had said that all conditions of benefit to the species presuppose at least its preservation, would he not have been given credit for meaning something that need neither be disputed nor confounded with the equally clear proposition that some conditions are conceivable in which existence is not a benefit; and in which therefore the destruction of a species is the only benefit remaining for it to receive?

I do not know what "Today" intends by its phrase "in the sense intended by the writer." The closely analytical minds of the editors of "Today " should note the collocation of words for the sense intended.

I submit that Spencer's argument is stated so as to imply no exceptions; in effect: (1) A is s convenience to B; but (2) B is included in A; therefore the preservation of A stands first for B. Now one fallacy may arise as to the mode of inclusion. Spencer is included in the British nation, but Spencer's existence does not depend upon the continued existence of the British nation. Again, in the "preservation of A," to avoid the fallacy we must adhere to all A, or at least to as much of A as includes B,—not resort to other some A. But A includes B, hence the elimination of B cannot be logically contemplated as a means of preserving all A. When a hen fights to the death for her chickens, does she fight on the supposition that all her species, including her own life, is threatened? I do not deny that she may do so, neither do I deny that her whole species is perhaps exposed to a danger. That is a question to be determined when we know whether or not the enemy would attack hens as well as chickens. I suggest that the hen may act under the influence of fallacious reasoning, and I would suggest the same thing of Spencer if he were giving indications of sacrificing himself for the British nation or for the human species, bearing his major premise in my mind. In order to overthrow his argument it is only necessary to establish a logical exception. I might have maintained simply that some benefits outweigh for the individual the consideration of preserving the species. Prospective benefits, as "Today" remarks, cannot be attained if life is surrendered, and medical ethics, for example, permits the sacrifice of the unborn child for the preservation of the mother, not merely in the cases of young mothers, but also in the cases of women who are not likely to be mothers again. (Surgeons are paid by the individual, not by the community.)

But my former writing was for the purpose of elucidating and establishing the Egoistic position, not for the purpose of merely gaining admissions of exceptions to the claims of Altruism, of which there is a strong flavoring added to facts with such phrases as "the order of obligation," and "is to be preferred." I have frankly admitted that "society" ought to prefer its own welfare to that of the individual if it is certain that they differ, as well as the individual ought to prefer his own welfare to all other things. Not many weeks ago "Today" followed closely what I had written on the force of this word "ought." Its illustration was so amusingly similar to the one which I had already put in print that I really believe "Today" had not seen my article in which that matter occurred.

As we agree in the use of this term, and as I find "Today" in the main not Altruistic (crazy), but only in a good sense altruistic with an altruism reducible by a rigid analysis to Egoism;

and as I hold intelligent Egoism to be incidentally in effect the truest altruism, I now use this word "ought" without fear of being misunderstood by "Today."

What does enthusiasm prove? That the crusader was more highly evolved than the rationalist? In one way, yes. Simply a fact. Nothing to cause evolution-worship in any thinking mind. Is not the political State, as we see it, vastly evolved? Are not its pretences largely related to altruism? On what ground do evolutionary Anarchists combat it? They are sometimes reminded that primitive barbarians have no State government and told by State Socialists that Anarchism appears to be an atavism. That seems to be the way in which "Today" treats philosophic Egoism, as I understand it,—a much mistaken way, I apprehend, for editors whose efforts are cheerfully directed to promote Individualism. Their own logic is on the road to Egoism. Their aim in politics is less sentiment, less self-sacrifice, a better balance of interests by their autonomy; but they do not understand that Egoism means all this in politics and as much in morals. "Today" has admitted Anarchism's claims as to the ultimate state of politics, not allowing itself to be radically misled by the appearance of involution, but seizing upon the fact of the evolution of the individual in politics. Probably it has not given equal study to Egoism, but, like others, has thought that the line of demarcation was of course drawn by us where the herd of preachers draw it. I never felt more Egoistic in getting something of the outside world *for* myself than I have always felt in spontaneously delivering something *of* myself to the outside world. The gist of our idea is not *I* against *you*, but I, and so you, *unawed*, — men conscious each one of his selfhood,—sovereign. This is the *Anarchy of morals*, subject to the same current misunderstanding as political Anarchy.

From an Egoistic point of view self-subordination, it will be readily perceived, is either a compliance with conditions, in which case it extends only as far as they dictate the necessity, or it is a fact of irrational conduct.

I am quite content to let "family" stand as a "convenient term,"—for an inconvenient arrangement. "Today" must be of very penetrating eye to see that the parent is "not the slave of his offspring," and yet that the parents "count themselves out, subordinate their welfare to the welfare of the family." "Today" is not required to define its terms or prove the compatibility of the two statements. If the parents are happy in doing as they do on their own premises, that should suit others passably well. If they are not happy, but go and sacrifice themselves,—I must procure a definition of the word "slave" before accepting "Today's" assurance without reserve. This is a touchy subject. The editors of "Today" are evidently devoted family men, and they have strong public sentiment with them. There are said to be some parents who are common slaves, and some who are willing slaves, but I am prepared to believe that it is possible to be a parent without being a slave, and on the other hand I think I have seen both men and women practically slaves in the marital relationship while not parents.

But I do not wish to be metaphysical. "Today" will excuse me. I should not know a metaphysician from any other kind of a physician if I met him in the street.

Whoever fails to distinguish between a mechanical principle and the engines which exhibit its operation may conceivably declare the principle annihilated when one or more of the engines are stopped by special friction. Such a person might assert that Egoism is knocked out because women must have babies and husbands must sit up at night to administer soothing syrup.

Tak Kak.

Wiles of the Social Man.

Liberty, vol. 8 no. 38 (May 7, 1892): 2.

Referring to *Liberty* of December 5, 1891, giving "To-Day's" article, "The Law and the Formula," and an editorial paragraph thereon, and now to "To-Day" of January 28, 1892, on "The State *vs.* the Man," I imagine that Mr. Tucker is not so well pleased with this latter article as with the former, and may be thinking with myself that "To-Day" has contrived after all to annex a considerable exception to that which it asserted to be complete without any.

At first it said: "The perfect and complete law of justice is already contained in the proposition, Every man is free to do that which he wills. The idea is absolutely complete."

Hereupon I outlined a chapter in which I shall discuss the imaginative character of the formula, its inherent limitations, and different shades of meaning in the predicate ac- cord-ing to the applications intended. Thus in one ordinary sense, the commonest in poll- tics, no man is permitted (free) to do whatever he wills. His "natural right" is not questioned. He encounters a proviso that he shall not exercise an aggressive freedom. This proviso, then, in the political sphere, describes a limitation.

But I was not prepared to find "To-Day" explaining away the subject. If the reader cannot rely upon the words "every man" as being unambiguous, what can he rely upon in discussion with Spencerians? In its last article, already referred to, it begins by saying that the law of equal freedom in its most general form is very simple, but "lends itself to easy misapprehension"; that antecedent considerations should be borne along; and speedily affirms: "The law of equal freedom is a social law. Inasmuch as some persons succeed in divesting the notion of man of nearly all its social connotations, the first circumscription of the idea of equal freedom is that it applies only to social men. Secondly, retaliation is excluded by the idea of equal freedom."

Who can beat such argument? The words "Every man" do not mean every man, but every social man! And what is so-cial? "To say that conduct shall be social is to intro- duce the assumption of equal freedom at once." Now is not this—apart from an incidental untruth—-precisely equal to saying that the original proviso was a limitation?

While the definition of society as a condition of equal freedom is gratifying as being an assurance that no great sacrifice of individual welfare is likely to be demanded by the ones who give this definition, I will only say here that it is an ideal, not the known society. Where the idealist says that I am no man if not a social man, the actual society man says that I shall have practically no freedom to do as I will, but only as society wills. Am I yet safe with the idealist? No, because to him I am not a man, for lack of the motive which makes "society," and, even were I a non-aggressive social man, he proposes to tax me. Take this statement of society from "To-Day:" "Society is a result of men's treating each other in a way different from that in which they severally treat the rest of nature. The difference consists in each man's ceasing to appropriate the faculties of others," etc. There seems to be implied something of a mystic tie. A little further on "To-Day" speaks of "a consciousness of duty to respect the rights of others," and it makes this a mainstay of society. From that to collective aggression upon the individual cannot be a long step, I think.

Apparently a non-aggressive disposition is not enough to propitiate the social oracle. "To-Day," having "circumscribed" the meaning of the law of equal freedom, examines some of the "ultimate deductions" from it, and states this one: "Every non-aggressive social man is justly free to do as he wills." See how we are conditioned. But soon it appears that the others in the majority make free to do as they will contrary to his will. "To-Day" says: "It has been said to follow that to prevent a non-aggressive social man doing as he wills is unjust. But it must be remarked that no series of syllogisms can make an affirmative proposition lead to a negative conclusion." Perhaps it has overlooked that in meaning there are three negatives in its latter proposition against one negative in the former, which leaves the propositions equal.

One more quotation without other comment than the suggestion that the careful review be extended to the propositions advanced by "social" men: "When we come to advance propositions about such a complex whole as a social man, it becomes necessary to review his attributes very carefully. It is not convenient to attempt the review here; but assumptions as to the nature of social men will be gradually introduced as their joint relations to the environment are defined."

TAK KAK.

Monopoly's Devious Ways.
Liberty, vol. 9 no. 29 (March 18, 1893): 3.

For cool, insolent, disingenuous statements nothing can sur-
pass the productions of the John Sherman class, the literary
and political agents of the money kings. An article by Comp-
troller Hepburn in the "North American Review" for March
is typical in its way. The subject is "National Banking and the
Clearing House."

I do not purpose going through all the argument, the aim
of which seems to be to persuade the public that to national
banks they might well look for more money of one kind, and
give up some of the money that now is, and it is assumed that
the public will find nothing amiss in spreading the losses by
insolvent banks upon the solvent, provided this be done by a
small tax.

I will content myself with quoting and remarking briefly
upon a few passages. Hepburn, regarding banks, says: "The
function of the government is to regulate by restraining. It
seeks to insure good banking by enforcing statutory prohibition against unsafe practices."

To regulate, by restraining? Let us see. Government regu-
lates weights and measures. Is restraint the primary idea in the
process? It may regulate by restraining, but that will gene- rally
be when it wants to restrain, and cloaks its action, otherwise
unauthorized, under the pretence of regulating.

Prohibition against unsafe banking? Primarily it has not
been so under the law of Congress which suppressed banks
of issue, for it destroyed the with the bad. There is abundant
and unimpeachable testimony that the State banks of New
York, Louisiana, and New England were as safe as the present
national banks. These are founded upon the plan of the better sort of State banks. The statutory prohibition struck down
banks quite safe and practices identical with those of Mr. Hepburn as a banker.

Now read what Hepburn says of silver: "The silver industry is entitled to no bounty. The policy of the government, in
purchasing a commodity which it does not want, for the sole
purpose of putting into circulation as money the obligations

given therefor, cannot be justified. An equally safe and more elastic currency can be otherwise provided."

This should be directed to Senator Sherman. The silver mining industry has not asked for a bounty, but for a return to the operation of the mint, to stamp without discrimination between different portions of the same metal. Whatever may have been the policy of "the government," it is no secret that the policy of the politicians of the gold privilege school, in forcing silver miners to accept purchase instead of free coinage, was to create the very cry and the very argument used by Hepburn and all his tribe,— that such purpose is improper. The Sherman act was passed in order to get the so-called Bland act repealed, and with the idea that the Sherman act, being less defensible in principle, could then be repealed, and this would leave free scope for the gold and bank-charter monopolists.

Mr. Hepburn, coming to State banks, incidentally airs his wisdom as a constitutional lawyer by asking: "Why should Congress delegate the question of bank circulation to the forty-four sovereignties that constitute the United States, with diverse laws, systems, and supervision?"

This is putting the horse behind the hansom. Congress is a body with delegated powers, or a usurping body, whichever Mr. Hepburn prefers. It is not expected therefore to delegate anything of importance. This may not apply to a "question."

The fact that Congress did not outright suppress banks of issue other than those of its own creation, but reached them by the foul blow of a ten per cent. tax, might have suggested to the receiver that the question with Congress was not what it should "delegate" of its own constitutional authority, but how it could manage to exercise a control which had not been delegated to it.

There are other remarks in Mr. Hepburn's article which tempt to criticism. One is that "the value of a currency depends upon the extent of country in which it possesses debt-paying power." If this be true without qualification, I must infer that it is impossible for Belgium to make a currency equal to Russian or Argentine shinplasters, and let the British Empire fall in pieces, the East India rupee will be more valuable than its nominal equivalent in British gold.

Is not Hepburn a free trader of a rather crazy sort? When one can get his wants supplied within a moderate distance, what does he want with buying from a greater distance and incurring debt that must be paid in currency at such distance? But if Hepburn is not a free trader, he argues at random, for certainly the circulation of money implies the circulation of products, and to place the consideration of a universal circulation of one money as the standard of its perfection is to contemplate not merely potential but actual far distant trade. Now, what is desirable should not be obstructed.

But Hepburn unwittingly condemns national bank currency, for it does not possess the debt-paying power of a legal tender note or of silver or gold coin of the government. And as for currency by consent, Mexican dollars are incomparably more widely acceptable than American bank notes or treasury notes. They are money throughout China, and they will pay a debt in any portion of the world in the same way as a British sovereign outside of its local legal tender sphere.

Tak Kak.

Spencer and George.— I.

Liberty, vol. 9 no. 31 (April 1, 1893): 2.

In beginning a few criticisms on the latest book by Henry George, entitled "A Perplexed Philosopher," it will be useful to state the purport of the argument. The introduction offers as a reason that Herbert Spencer—the philosopher in the case— enjoys a great reputation; that in his work on " Justice" he has changed his conclusion on private property in land, now affirming that it should continue; that people are led away by a great reputation: but George will restrict his discussion to Spencer's views related to the subject of landholding. It will be seen that the relation referred to is elastic. Thus George discusses as much as he sees fit of Spencer's views related to theology in order to force into some sort of relation with the land question the question of Spencer's moral obligation to truthfulness and self-sacrifice, or loss thereof by agnosticism. Then at the end of the book in the "moral" of the examination George hopes that the result may be "to promote freedom of thought." How has be adhered to his introductory resolution?

One inference from this state of case may be that George's introduction was written the first thing; but it is generally understood that introductions are written after the books to which they belong. George's may be no exception after all, for his language on page 6 is:

> I do not propose to discuss Mr. Spencer's philosophy or review his writings, except as embraced in or related to his teachings on one subject.

Writings related to "teachings" on a subject would be writings related to the subject, but George's purpose finds another relation. What then is the sense of the profession that the discussion shall be confined? There is a grave flourish of method about it, but the proponent, George, by not taking what Spencer calls related to one subject, but by taking what the proponent, George, relates to it in any way in his own mind, reserves the facility of making a point anywhere against his foe to weaken his inuence. He could have done that frankly, unless his nature is of another kind; but then he could not consistently use that profession that he did not purpose, etc.

George's work is on this plan: first to show by extracts from Spencer's earlier writings that Spencer was zealous at the outset in asserting that land belongs to society and not to individuals, and inviting society to assert its ownership through the State as the general landlord; that Spencer was then uncompromising in tone and eager to see the interest of the individual sacrificed to the will of God, making a virtue of this sentiment in the individual in common with George and all other Moralists. Years later, however, when Spencer had become a famed philosopher and substituted the unknowable and force for God, and evolution for religion, and when the land question was no longer one which the privileged classes could regard as harmless to their interest, however discussed, Spencer avowed that he had reconsidered his earlier views. By degrees he changed until he became a defender of the established order of things landed in Great Britain, and regarded the law of equal Liberty as being compromised by accrued claims in the matter of landed estates.

George says a good deal against Spencer's moral degeneracy, and devotes some effort to showing his shiftiness and cowardice.

George also dips into the godless philosophy and gives his readers a few specimens of the way he regards the argument. He does not mention Paley and the watch, but views the wonders of organic life as a steam engine or a telephone. If there is not intelligence visible in the user to account for all he sees, he infers that there was such intelligence in the mechanic.

George does not go into any inductions to offset the observations by which the theory of evolution may be supported. He makes a flying excursion into this domain and gets back to the land question. He winds up with a racy burlesque on Spencer's latest and lamentable position on land-owning and the compensation question, taking for comparison the imagined case of a northern abolitionist who had gone South, become comfortable among slaveholders, and been compelled to make his peace with them or take the consequences of their displeasure.

As Mr. Yarros some weeks ago anticipated, George makes a pitiable mess of attempting to discuss the Synthetic Philosophy,—that is, if one has regard to science, congruity of subjects, and enduring reputation; but the performance may be otherwise viewed if the aim is to make a popular book. It is not clear to my mind that George is of sufficient understanding to be set down as an unmixed humbug in this matter. I am willing to assume that it never occurred to him to think what would be his speculation on design if he found a machine with a contrivance inside operating to destroy the machine or frustrate its normal action.

Having given some account of Henry George's book, I will next present such arguments as strike me in reading certain passages. I shall accuse both Spencer and George of serious oversights, Spencer especially, in his earliest land doctrine, and shall point out that George has said the words necessary to essential corrections, but has failed to follow them up; also that George in this latest work has made certain crucial admissions.

Tak Kak.

Spencer and George.—II.

Liberty, vol. 9 no. 34 (April 22, 1893): 2–3.

In chapter 9, section 6, of his "Social Statics," published in 1850 but now withdrawn, Spencer wrote the following silly and contemptible fallacy:

> Either men have a right to make the soil private property or they have not.... If men have not such a right, we are at once delivered from the several predicaments already pointed out [as to equal rights and unequal possessions, quantity or quality of land]. If they have such a right, then is that right absolute, sacred, not on any pretence to be violated. If they have such a right, then is his Grace of Leeds justified in warning tourists from Ben Mac Dhui; ... then it would be proper for the sole proprietor of any kingdom... to impose just what regulations he might choose on its inhabitants.

This comes after an imaginary interview with a backwoodsman whom Spencer easily convicted of having squatted upon land belonging to Society, as all land, he declared, had been bequeathed by God to that body, otherwise called the human race. Society might therefore at any moment justly expel the backwoodsman. The latter pleaded a claim to compensation for improvements, and Spencer allowed the plea,—by analogy, he said, with the case of an occupant of a house belonging to another. (Curious idea of law, that a trespasser could recover compensation for his improvements.)

George is so intent upon reminding his readers that the Single Tax method in lieu of compensation—taking and reletting—had escaped Spencer's view, and upon what he declared an incongruous passage of Spencer's on compensation, and upon the difference between joint rights and equal rights, that he does not give any immediate attention to Spencer's foundation non- sense in the extract. Let us add a quotation from chapter 10, section 1, of "Social Statics." John Locke's remark was that, though the earth be common to all men, yet when one has mixed his labor with land, no man but he has a right to what is thus joined. On this Spencer said:

> The point to be debated is whether he had any right to gather or mix his labor with that which by the hypothesis previously belonged to mankind at large. The consent of all men must be obtained before any article can be equitably "removed from the common state nature hath placed it in."

That settles the matter, of course, as to acting *thus* "equitably," for the first men in various places would die, being unable to get either the consent or the refusal of all men to their occupancy of land; and all this comes directly from assuming that the earth belongs to Society, and not recognizing the fact that it belongs to those persons able to take it and hold it.

George, on the other hand, declares that Locke was not in error: "the right to the use of land is a primary individual right, not springing from society or depending on the consent of society either expressed or implied, but inhering in the individual and resulting from his presence in the world. Each man has a right to use the world because he is here and wants to use the world." The purport of this is clear, however nihilistic it may prove as to the doctrine of "rights." If being here and wanting to use a thing be the basis of right, how shall right be distinguished from might as illustrated in robbery or rape? It might be preferable to say that each man is under necessity to use the earth, and the idea that he should get permission from Society is a modern absurdity.

Spencer's declaration that right is "absolute, sacred, not on any pretence to be violated," contains something other than his definition and use of "rights" as the corollaries of equal Liberty. He admits expediency in allowing proprietors more than he says is their right. What is there but a moral bugbear to cause him to make the assertion that a right cannot be violated "on any pretence," — meaning for any reason? That is either nonsense or superstition. If his theory be admitted that the land belongs to all men in common, and if the majority permit the private proprietor to keep more than his right, they violate the right of all those who are dissatisfied with the concession.

Tak Kak's Liberty

George, agreeing with Spencer that men have equal rights to land, observes that Spencer has confused equal rights and joint rights. "When men have equal rights to a thing, as, for instance, to the rooms and appurtenances of a club of which they are members, each has a right to use all or any part of the thing that no other one of them is using.... But where men have joint rights to a thing,... then the consent of all the others is required for the use of the thing or any part of it by any one of them. Now the rights of men to the use of land are not joint rights; they are equal rights." Of course this leaves George's assertion of equal rights prior to convention merely an assertion. The club members are joint owners and have made an arrangement establishing the equal rights spoken of. I am prepared to maintain that, if men be regarded as joint owners of the earth, a similar arrangement with regard to it is the mod convenient and safe. George has committed his cause to the assertion that men's right to the earth is primarily an individual, and not a joint or social right; and, if he has failed by his analogy to show that equal rights exist without having their root in joint rights, he has nevertheless furnished a striking illustration of the expediency, even where joint ownership exists, of relegating the things to individual separate use. A corollary for Single Taxers will therefore be that the government must not violate the individual right to occupy land, even before it is surveyed and officially opened to settlement. The withholding of any area from settlement would make a wonderful difference in the rendered values of areas already settled compared with the acknowledgment of freedom to settle in advance of any permit or formality whatever.

I have touched on these points, and still reserve the subject of compensation and other matters, and pass over other discussions all the way from page 23 to page 236 of George's book in order to find what it seems to me should have come out like hot shot at the first assertion by Spencer, which I have alluded to as his foundation nonsense. When it does come from George (so far off), it is pointed rather to justify expropriation by the State than to demonstrate the fallacy of the reasoning in Spencer's dilemma of private property in land. Says George:

In our ordinary use of words everything subject

to ownership and its incidental rights is accounted property. But there are two species of property, which, though often ignorantly or wantonly confounded, are essentially different and diametrically opposed. Both may be alike in having a selling value and being subject to transfer. But things of the one kind are true property, having the sanction of natural right and moral law independently of the action of the State, while things of the other kind are only spurious property, their maintenance as property requiring the continuous exertion of State power, the continuous exercise or threat of its force, and involving a continuous violation of natural right and moral law…. Things which are brought into existence by the exertion of labor… are property of the first kind. Special privileges by which the State empowers and assists one man in taking the proceeds of another's labor are property of the second kind.

The principal idea here would have been a clear exposure of the wretched sophism with which Spencer started (see the first quotation in this article): either the soil may be private property or not; if it may, somebody may keep everybody else from using millions of acres. What rubbish! Either a person may have loaves of bread, beefsteaks, and water that are his own, or he may not; if he may, somebody may want to have all the loaves and beefsteaks and water in the world, and nobody else may eat or drink. By calling the connection of his Grace of Leeds with Ben Mac Dhui *property*, which, according to the true meaning of the word, it is not, —by calling robbery property it is attempted to scare or delude people into thinking that the settler who has well possessed and put his labor into a piece of ground is merely a tenant without just claim to stay there in defiance of the world; he may be justly expelled, said Spencer in his years of ghost-worship. The fact is that his Grace has never made the mountain private property. Let him inquire what *property* is, not what is called property.

What if a member of the club should undertake to occupy several chairs and tables, a couple of lounges, and be, as alleged by him, reading or going to read several periodicals? Would not the other members of the club have something to say in determining the *bona des* of occupancy? It seems to me that a long train of usurpations might give to the term occupancy such a spurious extension as to contradict its original meaning, and then a youthful philosopher Spencer could find occasion to write that either members have a right to "occupy" seats and "use" papers or not; that if the right to occupy seats and use or "read" papers be permitted, some member of the club who arrives first may occupy and be found reading or using all the seats, books, and papers in the club-house. If the right to occupy is, moreover, sacred, and the sacredness extends wherever the word is "used" (that is to say, abused), —as of course it does, for " sacredness" scarcely begins till words have attained greater power than facts,—there will be nothing for it but to leave the hog in possession. But if, on the other hand, people would reduce terms to their native significance, property would be no more terrible than occupancy, for that is just about what the word property really means.

Tak Kak.

Spencer and George.—III.

Liberty, vol. 9 no. 38 (May 20, 1893): 2.

In some instances George allows his desire to criticise Spencer such rein that he does not give full consideration to the propositions of the latter. For instance, on page 51 of " A Perplexed Philosopher " he refers to Spencer's observation in " Justice" on weapons, instruments, dress, and decorations as being, with food, things in which property is first recognized, and quotes: " When with such articles we join huts, which, however, being commonly made by the help of fellow-men who receive reciprocal aid, are thus less distinctly products of an individual's labor, we have named about all the things in which, at first, the worth given by effort is great in comparison with the inherent worth." George introduces a severe criticism on Spencer's use of the term value with the phrase: "Passing the queer notion that things made by two or more men are *less distinctly* products of an individual's labor than things made by one man." So far from the notion being queer, everybody but George will agree that community aid in building a but leaves the individual possessor much less distinctly the owner than he is of the things which he has made without such aid. Such a point may serve as a test of George's reach and circumspection as a critic.

One should not expect entire consistency in the author of "Social Statics," since his principle led him to assert that the settler may be justly expelled; yet he says not without payment for improvements. When, therefore, we reach sec. 9, chap. 9, which George labors over as an "incongruous passage," would it not be better to assume, as it seems to show, that a further fact had made its impress on Spencer's mind than to try with George to remove the incongruity by reading into the passage words that are not there? George calls the section a "weak and confusing spot," the reason for which view on his part will become plain. The section is as follows:

> §9. No doubt great difficulties must attend the resumption, by mankind at large, of their rights to the soil. The question of compensation to existing proprietors is a complicated one,—one that perhaps cannot

be settled in a strictly equitable manner. Had we to deal with the parties who originally robbed the human race of its heritage, we might make short work of the matter. But, unfortunately, most of our present landowners are men who have either mediately or immediately — either by their own acts or by the acts of their ancestors— given for their estates equivalents of honestly- earned wealth, believing that they were investing their savings in a legitimate manner. To justly estimate and liquidate the claims of such is one of the most intricate problems society will one day have to solve.

Unwilling to admit the obvious fact,—that Spencer has here stated and admitted a distinctive claim against Society, based on its encouragement of investments,—and in the teeth of Spencer's declaration that the question of compensation is a *complicated* one, George proposes to remove the complexity by reading into the passage, after "compensation," the words, "for their improvements," and after "estates," the words, "which include many inseparable improvements." Now, it cannot be denied that, when one pays his money on the faith of law and public policy for an unimproved estate, one has parted with value just as truly as when one pays it for an improved estate. Moreover, if the matter referred to were not this investment feature, why should Spencer say that it makes such difference that the present landholders are not the original ones? Compensation for improvements, he had said, would be due to the original holders. Something more, he says, is due to "most of our present landowners." He has in fact come across the same principle as investment in government bonds or any other act of confidence in the political sovereignty; but George refuses to follow and attempts to keep the land question from that complication. George holding Spencer by the coat-tail becomes farcical. For the Single Taxer, who puts the government forward as the practical equivalent of all mankind for the purpose of collecting the rent, would be horrified to perceive that the government acting as the same equivalent had bargained and sold the interest of all living mankind in a particular estate. Is its authority so easily assumed without evidence of delegation for the purpose of collecting annually, but not for the purpose of selling, hypothecating, or leasing for "longer term than one year"?

If the settler has not obtained an authorization from all mankind, neither has any existing government obtained it. If we have bought of a government, we have a question to raise when that agency assumes to represent " all mankind." Either it is their agent or it is not. Mr. George can take either horn of the dilemma. If it is their true representative, we will hold them to its conveyances. If it is not their true agent, we protest against paying it the rent which by the hypothesis belongs to them.

In my next paper I purpose going further into the subject of compensation, and exposing a huge inconsistency and fallacy on the part of George on that subject.

TAK KAK.

Cleveland's Commission.

Liberty, vol. 9 no. 51 (April 21, 1894): 2–3.

One of the most pitiable exhibitions in the whole range of political organizations of any time is the Democratic party at the present hour, and I am greatly mistaken if a considerable number of its members do not keenly feel that such is the fact.

To go no further back than Tilden and 1876, the party took its stand upon free trade and free coinage of silver. I say free trade, without allowance for such forced mode of speech as trimmers and equivocal politicians resort to. It was proposed to raise revenue, and trade was not indeed to be free as we Anarchists would have it, but there were to be no duties for protection. England is called a free trade country in the ordinary acceptation of the term, which is antithetical to a protective tariff. The wriggling of small or great politicians has not changed the term free trade, *libre échange*, *Freihandel*. Why do not the ridiculous quibblers ring the changes on free coinage by contending that it would not be free if there were a charge to cover the cost of labor in coinage? The policy of *exclusion* in either instance is the chief characteristic, the presence of which determines the use of language, – protection of the gold standard, protection of domestic industries. The owners of silver would cheerfully pay the cost of coinage, and most of the Democratic consumers of imported goods would as cheerfully pay some rate of taxation for the support of that imaginary creature, — as far as this country is concerned, – "a government economically administered." From Tilden to Cleveland the history of the Democratic party is the story of a political organization with two economic proposals, one of which it steadily adhered to, but the other of which suffered partial eclipse in Hancock and Randall. Congress, under Democratic inspiration, repeatedly snubbed presidents and their veto power on the silver question. Finally Cleveland came on the scene and immediately after his first election drove full tilt against the free coinage doctrine. Then his party began to waver. It had the power to place itself on record during the Harrison administration as before, but before the last presidential election the faction opposed to free coinage had succeeded in compromising the sincerity of the party.

The manoeuvering on the approach of the presidential contest took the guise of an insidious counsel to concentrate on one issue. The free coinage men were offered assurances that after securing tariff-reform their day would come. While this lying pretence was being used, the national banks and lawyers in their employ were quietly stocking the conventions in the Democratic free silver states. They procured the sending to the last national convention at Chicago of delegations which simply betrayed the confidence of the great majority of their constituents and assisted to make, or passively submitted to, a jumbo plank, serviceable for no purpose but juggling. This could not have been done without putting the silver question out of sight, as if it were too well understood to need discussion among Democrats. Their whole attention was directed to the tariff.

Cleveland elected, it was somewhat of a shock to the Western and Southern Democrats to learn gradually that the tariff wasn't the first and only question after all, but that silver coin- age must be got out of the way by knocking in the head all aspirations on that subject. Now, however, they know the whole damned scheme by its fruition, and it rests with each to decide whether his attachment to a name and organization is greater than his disgust with the non-representative character of a national political organization whose objective points are the spoils of office for the political jackals and the spoils of monopoly for the pullers of convention and congressional wires, the privileged employers of the jackals.

If such are not the reflections of hundreds of thousands of sincere Democrats, I am in error simply as to the number. I look confidently for accessions to the adherents of Liberty, though doubtless more will for the present go into the Populist camp. But a number of these tell me they do not believe in all the doctrines of Populism. They are going into that movement to cooperate in accomplishing only certain things, or, let us say, perhaps for political revenge. What those people need is an opportunity to read *Liberty* and other publications in its line.

As for the Democratic party, the maxim applies: False in one, false in all. It is shaping as falsely on free trade as on free coinage. Lest the reader suppose that I am surprised at this, I will say that I am not and have not been so. I earnestly desired that the party should have an opportunity of showing its quality. The mass of the people who support it are politically honest, as qualified by the usual amount of prejudice in all swayed by the fealty idea in any shape. Their eyes could not be opened without the object lesson, and there it is. If we give five per cent. to Liberty, it will be something to congratulate ourselves upon, and Cleveland, like Carnegie, will not have lived in vain. Populism next, and I think we may gain fifteen per cent. on that turn.

Tak Kak.

A Pointer for Trade Unions.

Liberty, vol. 14 no. 12 (August, 1903): 4.

John McKean, a lawyer of Springfield, Mass, writes as follows in "Medical Talk" for June, 1903:

> Until about a year ago I was perfectly indifferent to the state of medical legislation in our State. But at about that time I was called upon to defend a "Magnetic and Biochemic Physician," who had been arrested for practising his profession without a certificate from the medical board.
>
> I thereupon studied into the question, not only in our commonwealth, but in many others of the States. I am of opinion that the statute in our State is unconstitutional as class legislation, and so advised my client. It was decided to take the case to the supreme court of the State and test the question. But, seeing our attitude, the matter was dropped by the representative of the medical board who [had] caused the arrest of my client, and "no bill" was found by the grand jury.
>
> At a recent hearing before the public health committee of the Massachusetts legislature on a bill to repeal the medical board statute, I stated before the committee that the law was unconstitutional; that I had a client (whom I produced before them) who had been arrested under this law, and who desired to take the matter up, but could not, because the medical board dared not carry it up; I dared the medical board to take a case to the supreme court and test the question. I told them to their face they were afraid to do so; told them we would furnish the defendant and evidence. My client told the committee that he was practising contrary to the statute; that he intended to continue to do so; that he would furnish the names of one hundred more who would make the same statement; and yet, in the face of this, no action of any kind had been taken by the medical board.
>
> What kind of a law is this that can be and is with

impunity defied in the very cradle and home of legislation, the State House at Boston, and before the very lawmakers themselves?

What a travesty of justice it is that such a law is allowed to remain as a bugaboo for weaklings, who dare not defy it! A law that was conceived in trickery, was born in iniquity, and bears patent on its face the marks of its conception and birth.

And yet there it stands and must stand apparently. The legislature won't change it, and the judiciary can't get a chance at it.

The "Eclectic Medical Gleaner" for July gives a summary of the above statement, and appends its own editorial opinion in the following words:

In our opinion the medical law of Massachusetts is no exception. An untrammeled court will, in many States, completely upset medical legislation, if given the opportunity. We believe them all to be "class legislation" and contrary to the constitution of the United States.

I have not seen or heard the arguments of lawyers on the subject of this class legislation; but certainly it looks very much as if the trade unions might aspire to have laws passed authorizing the governor to appoint for each trade a board composed exclusively of members of the union. which board shall have power to certify who is and who is not qualified to work at each trade, with a penalty upon any one working without a certificate from the trade board. There are none but doctors on the medical hoards,—none but unionist doctors.—and only three schools of doctors are recognized in the medical registration laws,—mostly enacted within the past few years and now covering all the States.

Of course the power which was sought under pretext of protecting the public health was soon abused for professional interest. The president of the Indiana regular board announces that physicians arriving from other States and desiring to practise in Indiana may be admitted to registration without re-examination, provided they have diplomas and come with evidence of legal registration and good professional conduct in the State of their former residence, and provided that all such physicians so excused from re-examination shall make oath that they have not been and will not become traveling practitioners.

The Texas eclectic medical examining board refused license to a prominent advertising doctor, a graduate of the reputable Cincinnati college of its own school, solely because he advertises. The last I read of the matter, he had applied to the State supreme court for the writ of mandamus to compel the examining board to issue to him a certificate of license.

Those protective professional laws are of recent adoption in the Western and Southern States, but they had existed in some Eastern States for years. It is now ten or eleven years since the medical boards of Pennsylvania deliberately excluded a New England physician of first-class collegiate standing, a graduate A. B. of Dartmouth, M. D. of the National College (regular) of Washington, D. C., 1864, and Dean of the Vermont Medical College, a gentleman in every way as learned and skilled in medicine and surgery as the best of the Pennsylvania University professors. The regulars would not have him because he did not give calomel. The eclectic board balked, and declined to examine him. His offence consisted in his efforts to spread education among the people, as to health and medicine. The board examiners virtually admitted that the applicant knew all that they knew. They suggested that a promise of "conformity" in practice was expected. He had no such trade-union promise to give.

Let it not be supposed that I have any spite against trade unions. They are respectable till they take the law or any other invasive weapon to beat down competitors.

TAK KAK.

"Representative" Government.
Liberty, vol. 14 no. 13 (September, 1903): 4.

Italian newspapers sometimes intimate that the Maltese speak Italian or are Italians, but much oftener they say that Malta belongs to the Italian-power. That is to say, "of right,"—of the right which is not at present might. Whether there will be any Italian power when reason shall be right and might is a question which does not occur to them. It would be a stretch for the burgher imagination, of any nationality, to entertain even the limited ideal that a small island belongs "of right" to its inhabitants collectively, sorry substitute as this is for the ideal of individual Liberty and possession.

The British newspapers state that the Maltese dialect is compounded chiefly of Arabic, "but has always been considered too imperfect for legal or professional use;" that "the native Maltese are not a European race, and have never been a part of any continental people. They constitute in every sense a separate and miniature nationality of their own."

It was thought by both the British authorities and the elected members of the Maltese council that either English or else Italian must be used in the courts and taught in the schools. The elected members had a majority, and they have stood lately for making the study of Italian compulsory in the public schools. So now the British government, after having governed with- out the consent of the elected members, through a peculiar clause in the constitution, has amended the constitution, and thereby reduced the number of elected members from thirteen to eight, and increased the appointed members from six to nine. On the face of such a statement it seems that representative government has been simply suppressed, and that merely a talking representation is continued in the council. However, when we reflect that representative government in Europe is not even professedly universal suffrage, but is done by the property-qualification vote of a minority of the inhabitants, we need not flatter ourselves that we have reached any true idea regarding where the greater misrule lies when civic authorities clash, and such a seemingly gruff overriding of the "popular will" occurs.

It is not improbable that Italian property-owners have counted for much more than their numerical relation to the rest of the inhabitants, the less thrifty Maltese. It is declared by the "Yorkshire Herald" that a preference for the English language over Italian "has been expressed by ninety per cent. of the parents." That English newspaper adds: "It is gratifying to think that the government will now be able to give effect to the popular choice."

Oh! where are we when we talk of "representative government"? Surely governments always represent those who govern. Masks off when it comes to the exercise of force.

Tak Kak.

The Virus of Specific Moralism.

Liberty, vol. 14 no. 14 (October, 1903): 7.

To the Editor of *Liberty*:

That specific moralism is an insanity I believe to be a truth which will impress itself upon every observer, candidly open to entertain such an idea and willing to note the temper of specific moralists in controversy. Their misrepresentations are usually in direct ratio as their zeal. When I have a tilt with any of the class and the editorial umpire threatens to expurgate the moralist's remarks, but does not, I am inwardly thankful that he permits the full exhibition; for all you want to do with a specific moralist is to stir him up by candidly stating that you regard his belief as fanaticism, and he goes wild with rage. This will apply to all those cases in my experience.

Tak Kak.

STANDARD FREETHOUGHT WORKS

BLOOD & VOLTS—*Th. Metzger* $16
CONFESSIONS OF A FAILED EGOIST—*Trevor Blake* $10
ELBERT HUBBARD'S THE PHILISTINE—*Bruce A. White* $16
HOMO 99 AND 44/100 NONSAPIENS—*Gerald B. Lorentz* $18
MIGHT IS RIGHT: THE AUTHORITATIVE EDITION—*Ragnar Redbeard* . . . $20
MIGHT IS RIGHT: 1927 FACSIMILE EDITION—*Ragnar Redbeard* $16
THE OCCULT TECHNOLOGY OF POWER—*The Transcriber*. $8
THE PHILOSOPHICAL WRITINGS OF EDGAR SALTUS—*Edgar Saltus* . . . $18
THE RADICAL BOOK SHOP OF CHICAGO—*Kevin I. Slaughter* $16
THE RED SECT—*Enzo Martucci*. $16
RIVAL CAESARS: A ROMANCE...—*Ragnar Redbeard* $20
THE SATANIC SCRIPTURES—*Peter H. Gilmore* $17
SORCERIES AND SCANDALS OF SATAN—*Henry M. Tichenor*. $15
STRONG SONGS OF THE DEAD—*Th. Metzger*. $16
THIS UGLY CIVILIZATION—*Ralph Borsodi* $20

BENJAMIN DeCASSERES SERIES:
ANATHEMA! LITANIES OF NEGATION $10
FANTASIA IMPROMPTU & FINIS $16
FULMINATIONS: CAUSTIC, COSMIC, CAPRICIOUS $16
IMP: THE POETRY OF BENJAMIN DeCASSERES. $15
NEW YORK IS HELL: THINKING AND DRINKING IN THE BEAUTIFUL BEAST $18
SPINOZA: LIBERATOR OF GOD AND MAN & AGAINST THE RABBIS . . . $15
THE BOY OF BETHLEHEM—Bio DeCasseres (Hardbound) $23
THE SUBLIME BOY—*Walter DeCasseres* $7

THE PORTABLE L.A.ROLLINS SERIES:
THE MYTH OF NATURAL RIGHTS $15
LUCIFER'S LEXICON. $15
OUTLAW HISTORY $15

PAMPHLETS

BOVARYSM: THE ART-PHILOSOPHY OF JULES DE GAULTIER—*Wilmot E. Ellis* $4
IMMORALITY AS A PHILOSOPHIC PRINCIPLE—*Paul Carus* $5
MAX STIRNER AND THE PHILOSOPHY OF THE INDIVIDUAL—*Leo Markun* .$8
MAN-EATING AND MAN-SACRIFICING—*Anon*. $3
THE NIETZSCHE MOVEMENT IN ENGLAND—*Oscar Levy*. $2
PRIMITIVES: POEMS AND WOODCUTS—*Max Weber*. $6

UNDERWORLD AMUSEMENTS
444 MARYLAND AVE. #7940   ESSEX, MD 21221
For postage add $4 for the first item, $1 for each additional.
Or visit WWW.UNDERWORLDAMUSEMENTS.COM

Made in the USA
Middletown, DE
16 August 2024